Angels Over Macon

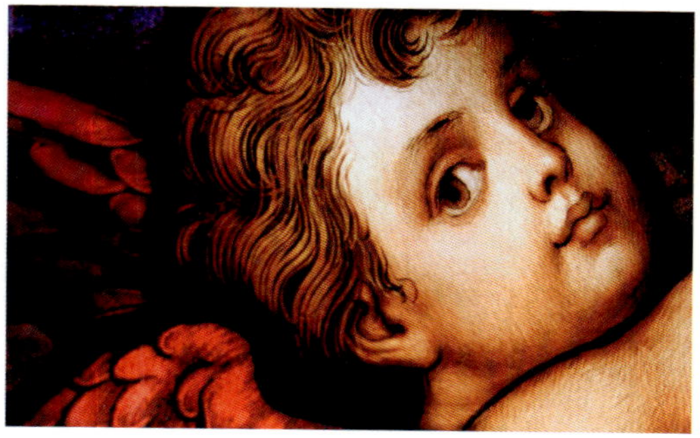

"Life is sweet where angels dwell."

Macon, Georgia, is a fortunate city to be home to so many angels and I have been blessed to have had the opportunity to come face to face with so many of them.

All of the angels in this book were photographed in churches and cemeteries in downtown Macon. I hope this book inspires you to seek them out for yourself. Life truly is sweet where angels dwell.

Maryann Bates

Indigo Publishing Group, LLC

Publisher	Henry S. Beers
Associate Publisher	Richard J. Hutto
Associate Publisher	Rick Nolte
Executive Vice President	Robert G. Aldrich
Operations Manager	Gary G. Pulliam
Editor-In-Chief	Joni Woolf
Designer	Maryann Bates
Director of Marketing and Public Relations	Mary D. Robinson
Distribution	Nick Nolte

Printed in China

Library of Congress Control Number: Data in process

ISBN: (10 Digit) 1-934144-23-1
(13 Digit) 978-1-934144-23-7

Indigo Publishing Group books are available at quantity discounts with bulk purchase for educational, business, or sales promotional use. For information, please write to: Indigo Publishing Group, SunTrust Bank Building, 435 Second Street, Suite 320, Macon, GA 31201 or call 866-311-9578.

"I saw an angel in the marble
and carved until I set him free."

Michelangelo

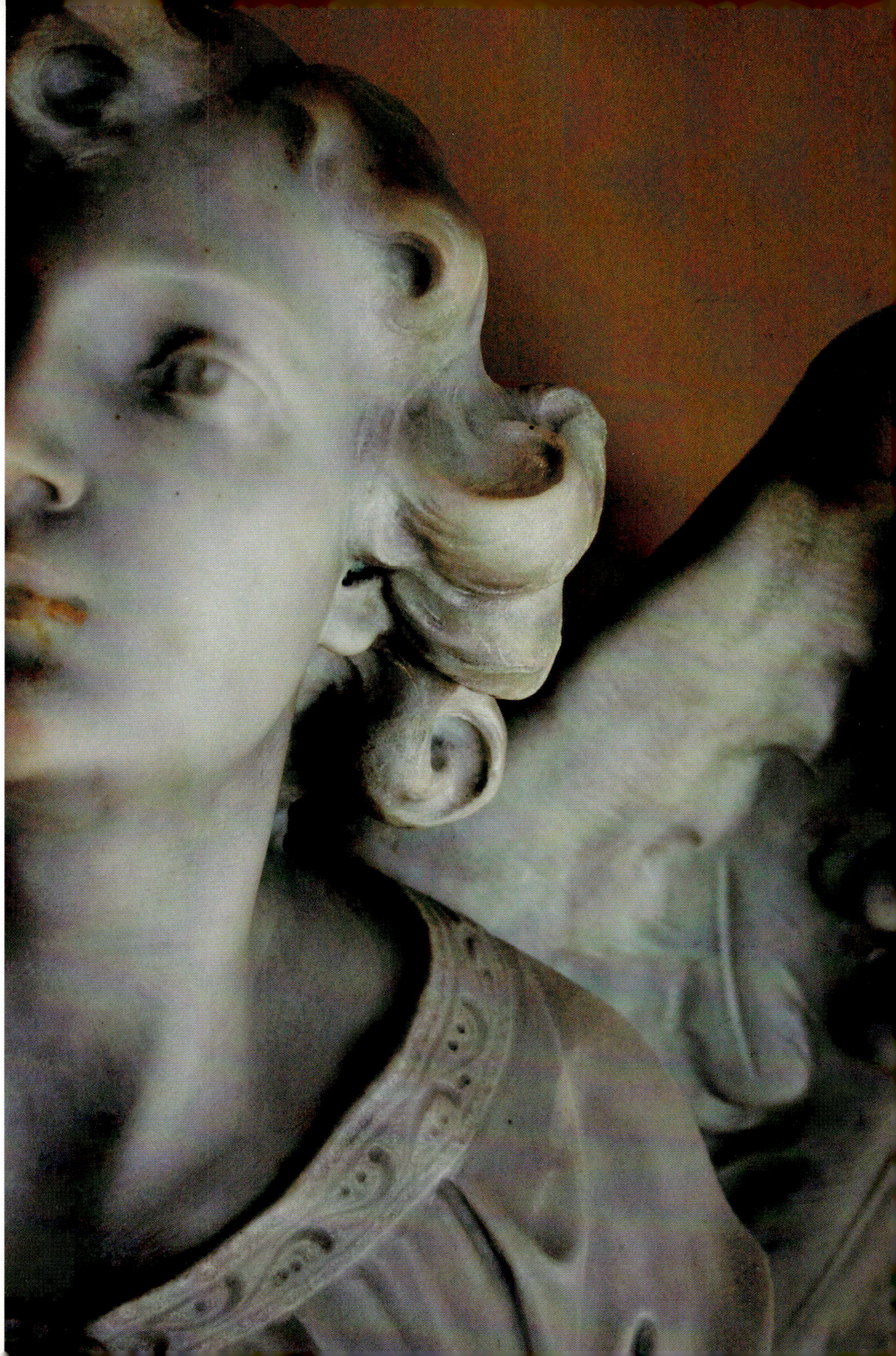

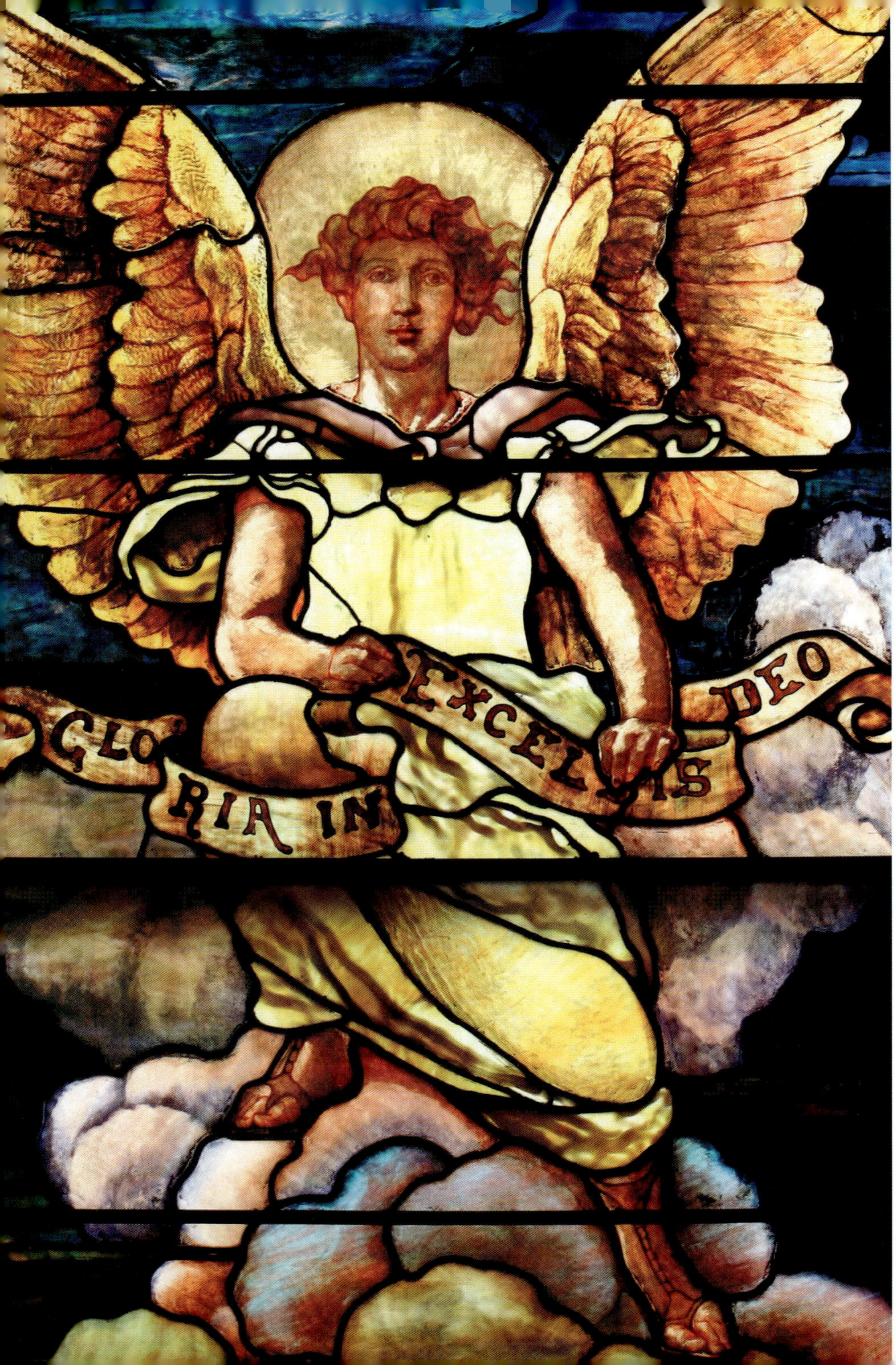

"Angel strong,
Angel bright,
Keep us safe
throughout the night.

Wake us with
the morning sun,
Walk with us,
'Til our work is done."

M'anni Dela Beech

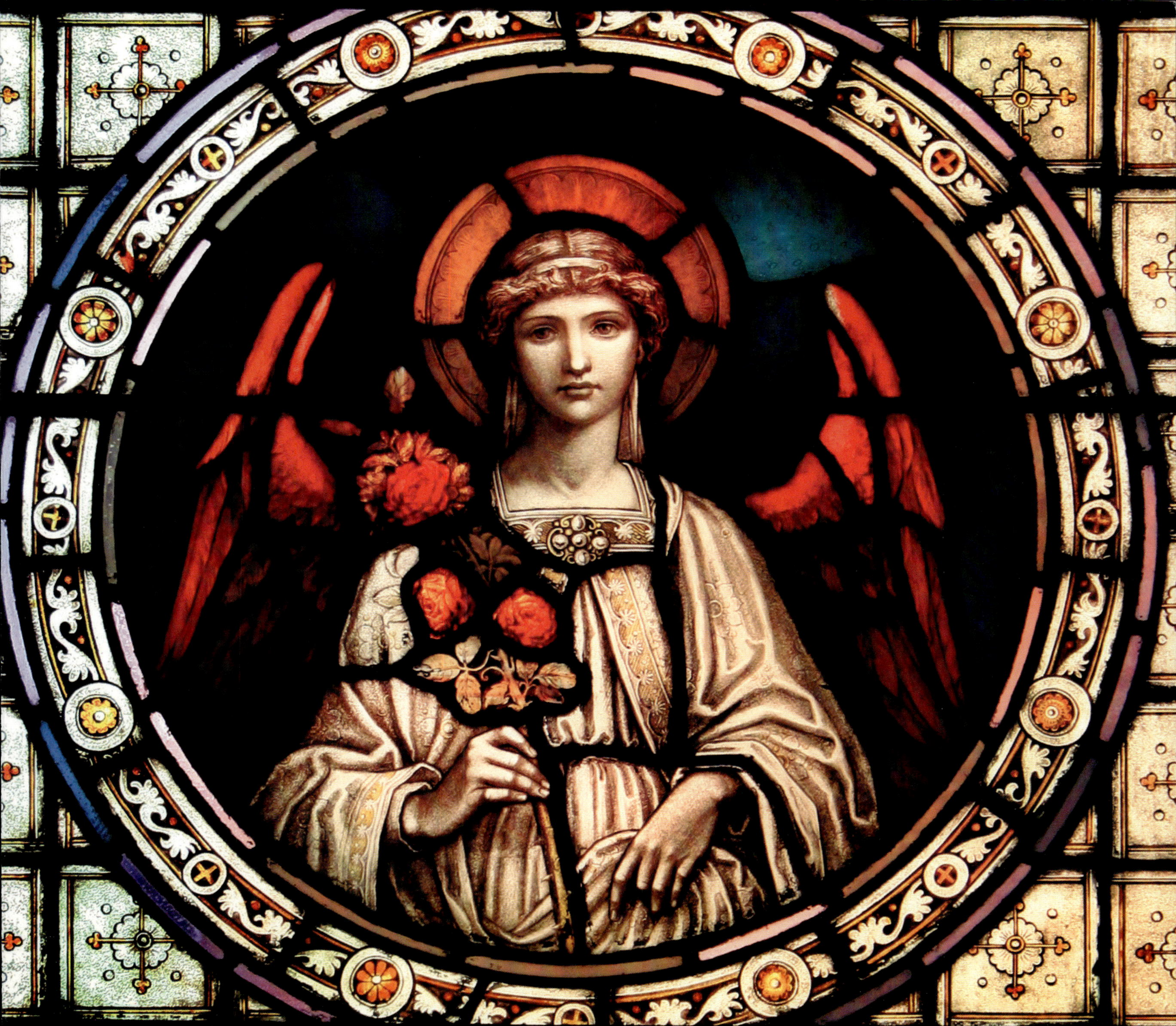

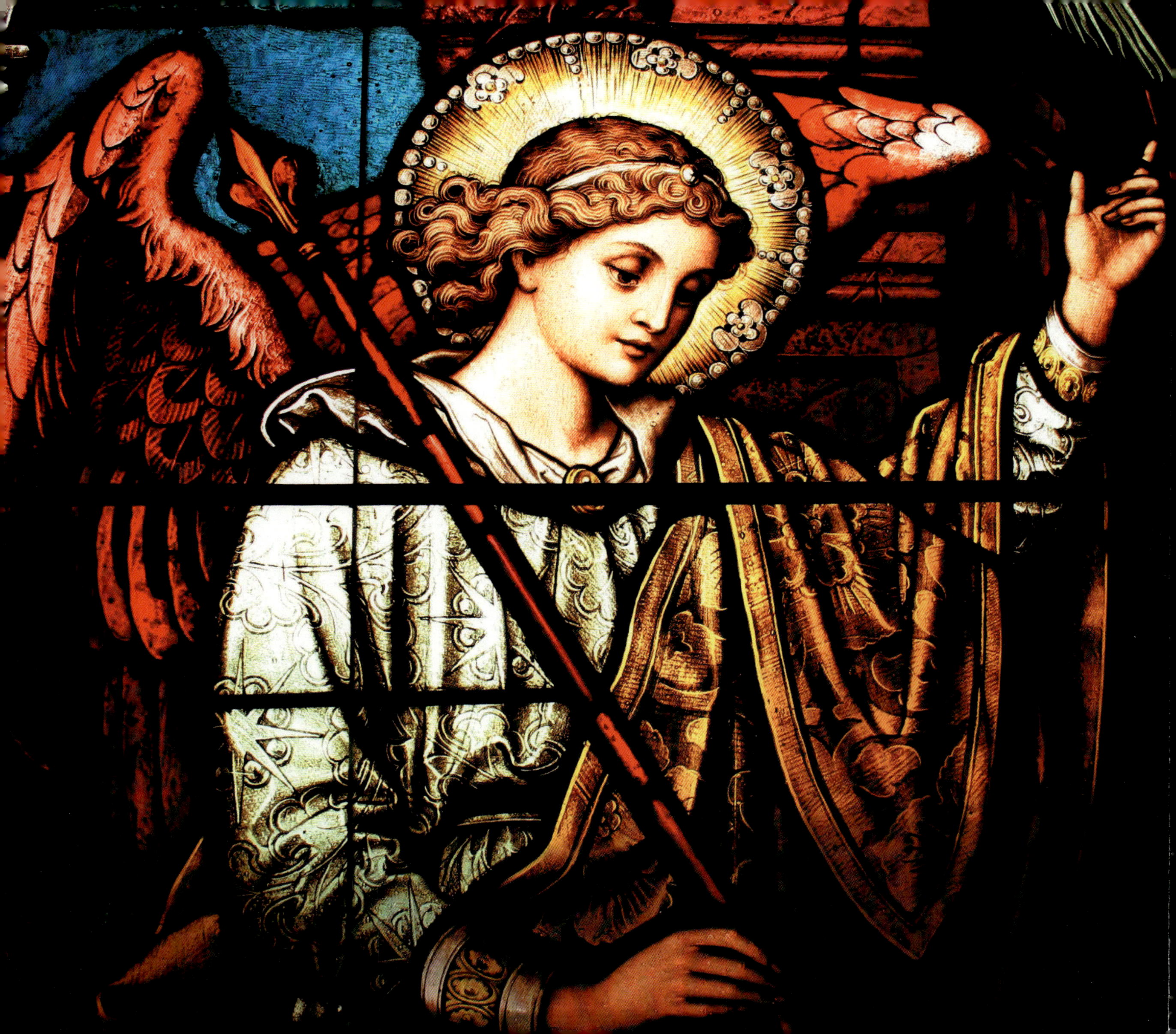

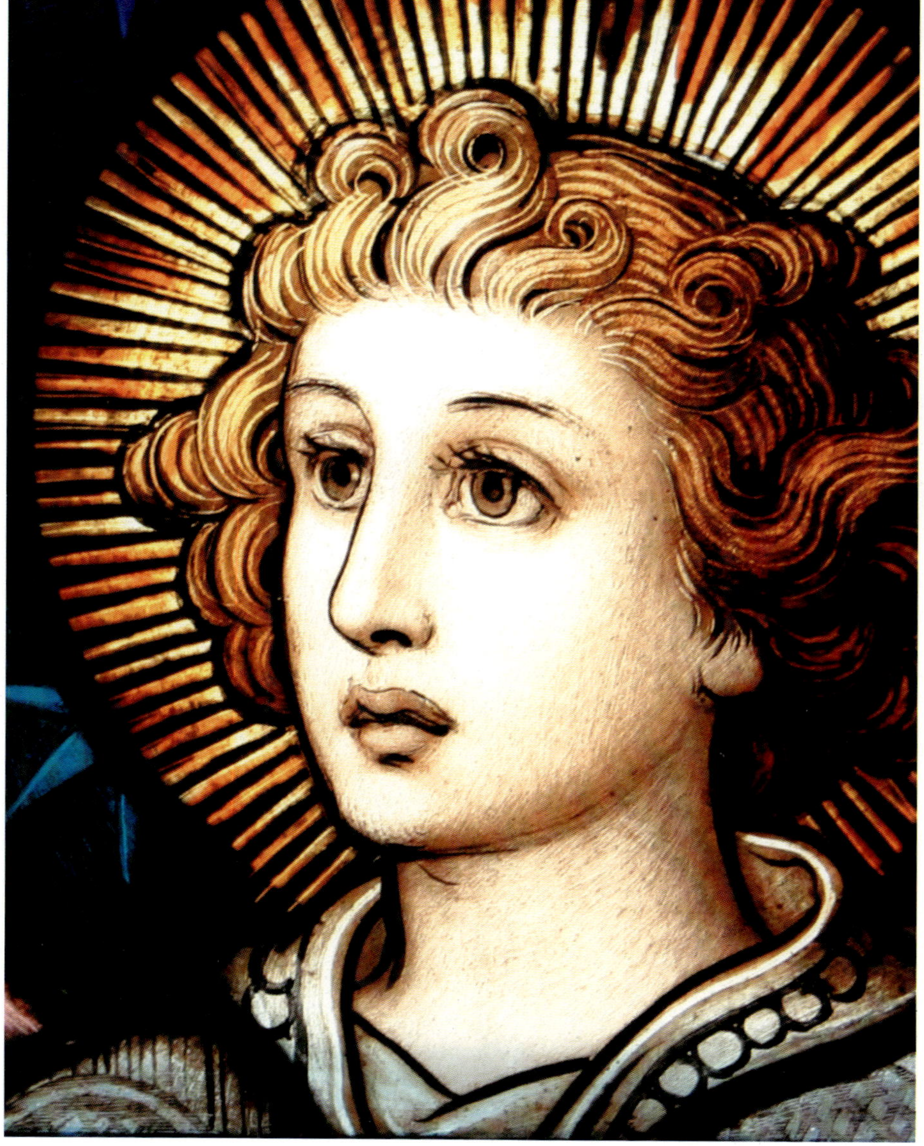

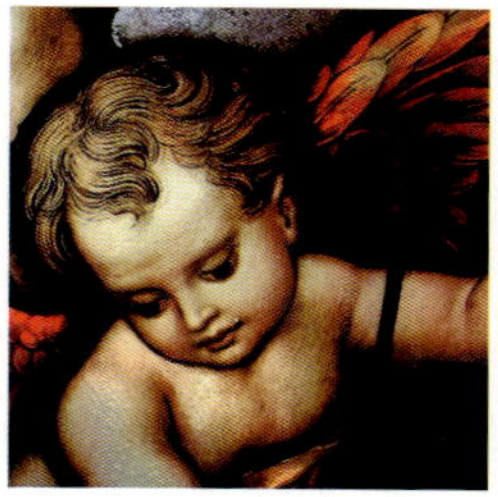

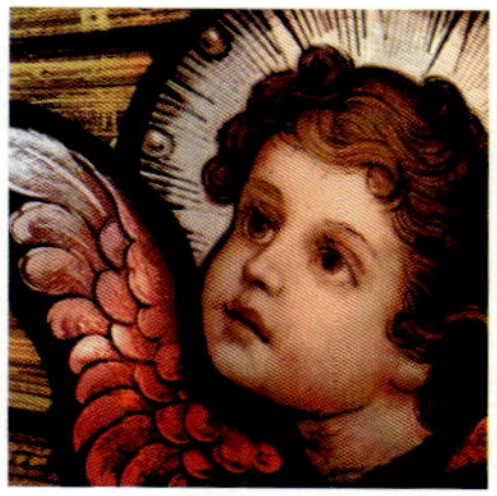

"While we are sleeping, angels have conversations with our souls." Anonymous

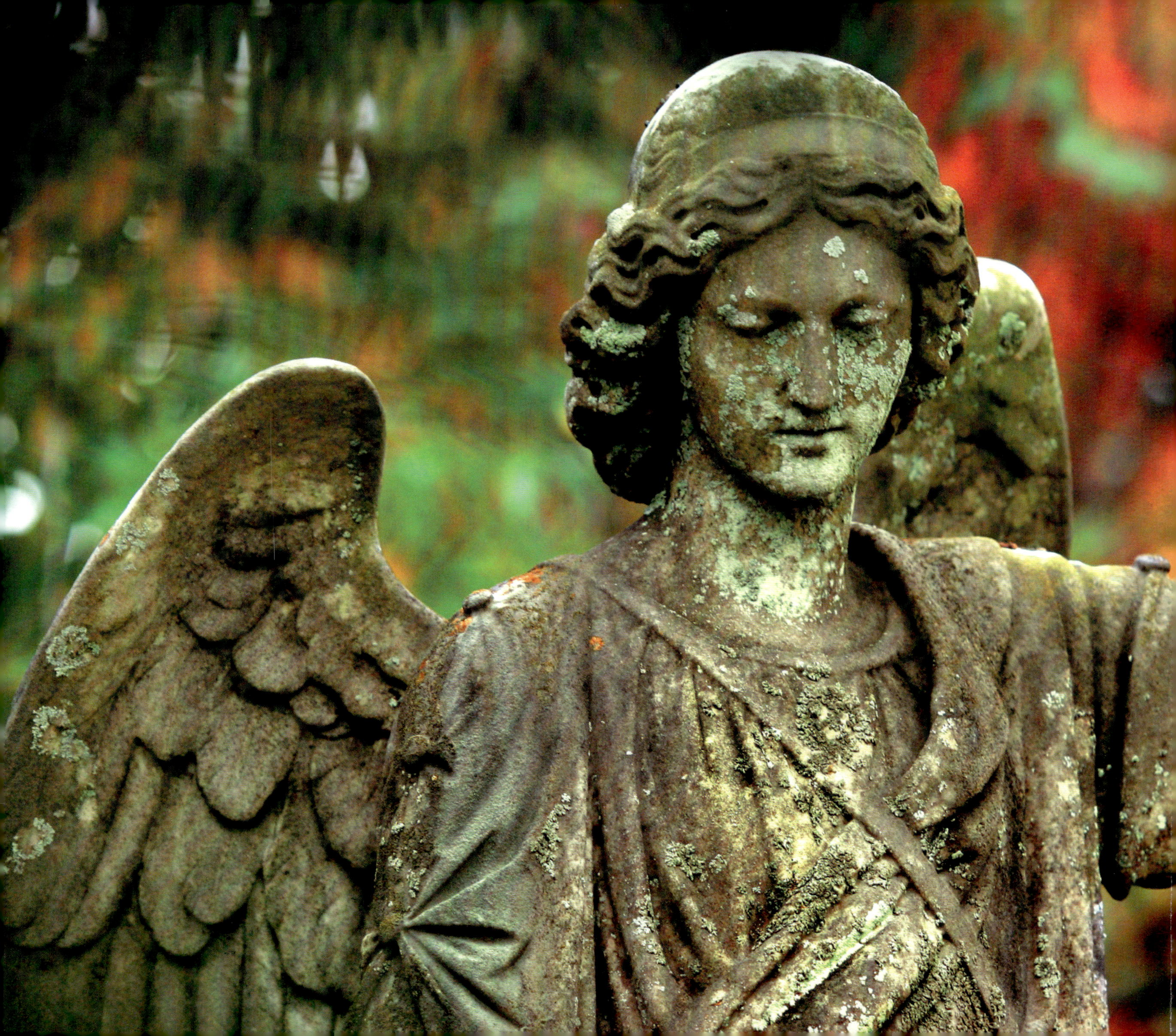

"Ever felt an angel's breath
in the gentle breeze?
A teardrop in the falling rain?
Hear a whisper amongst
the rustle of leaves?
Or been kissed by a
lone snowflake?
nature is an angel's
favorite hiding place."

Carrie Latet

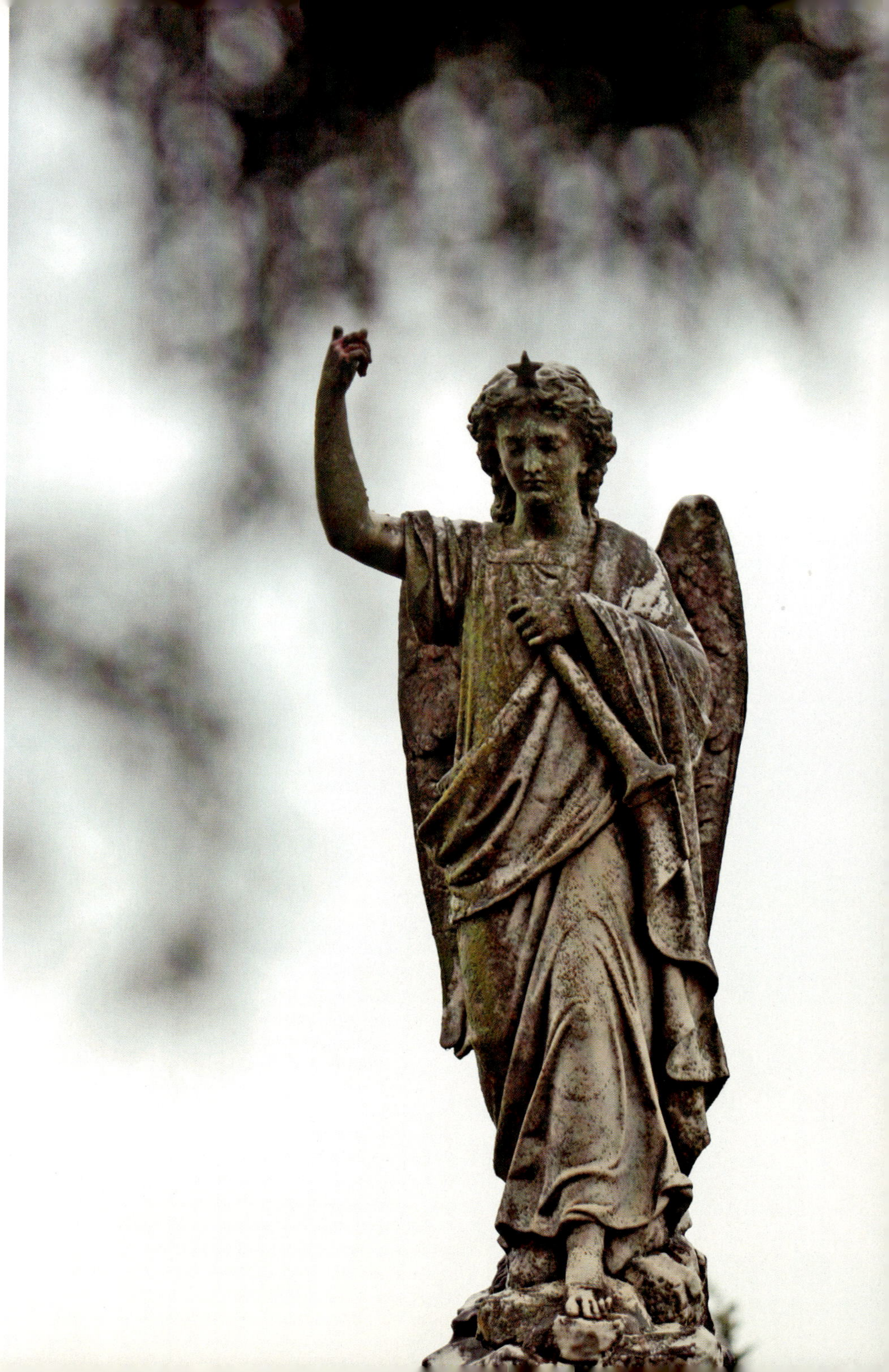

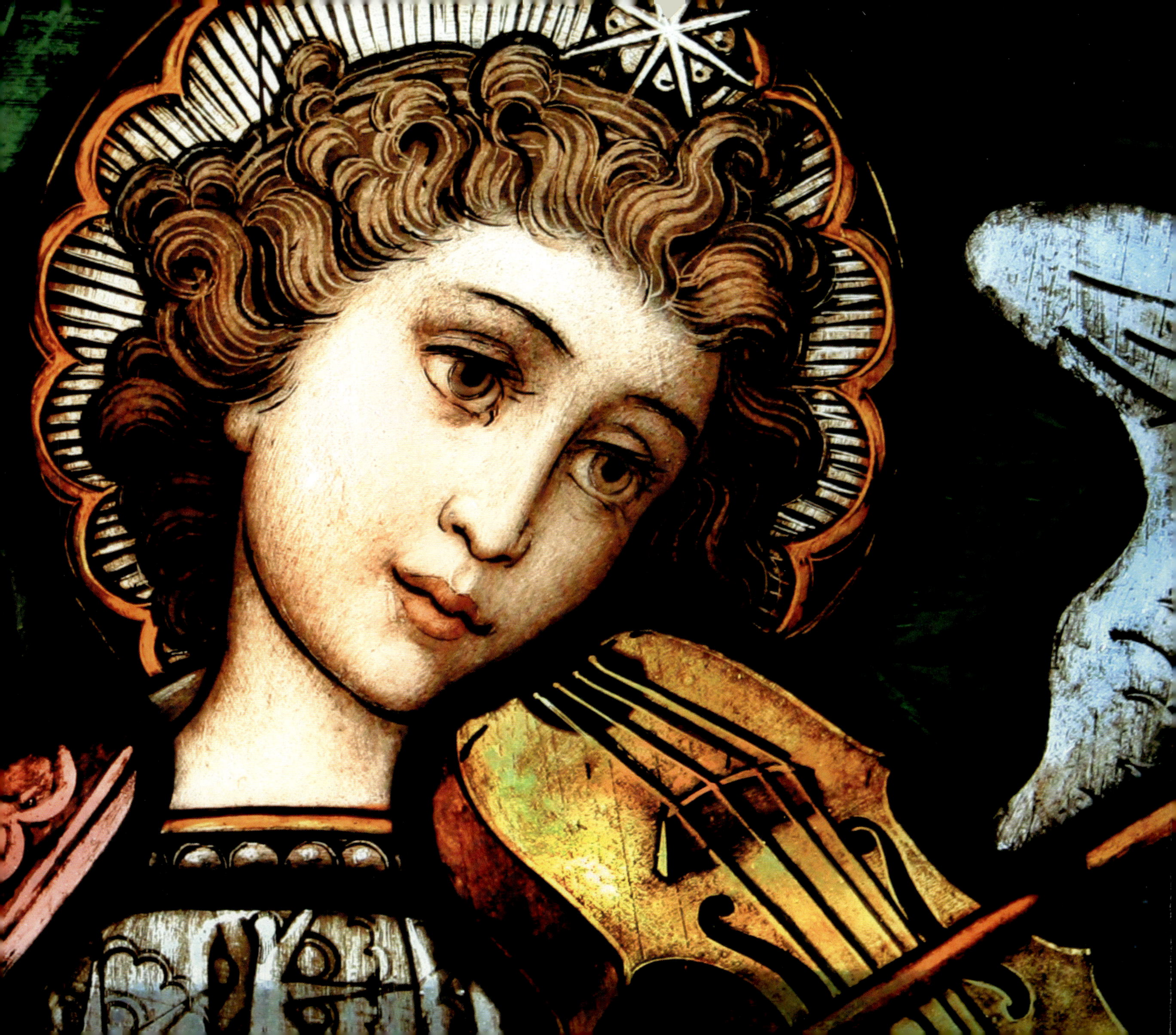

"Music is well said to be
the speech of angels."

Meriel Stelliger

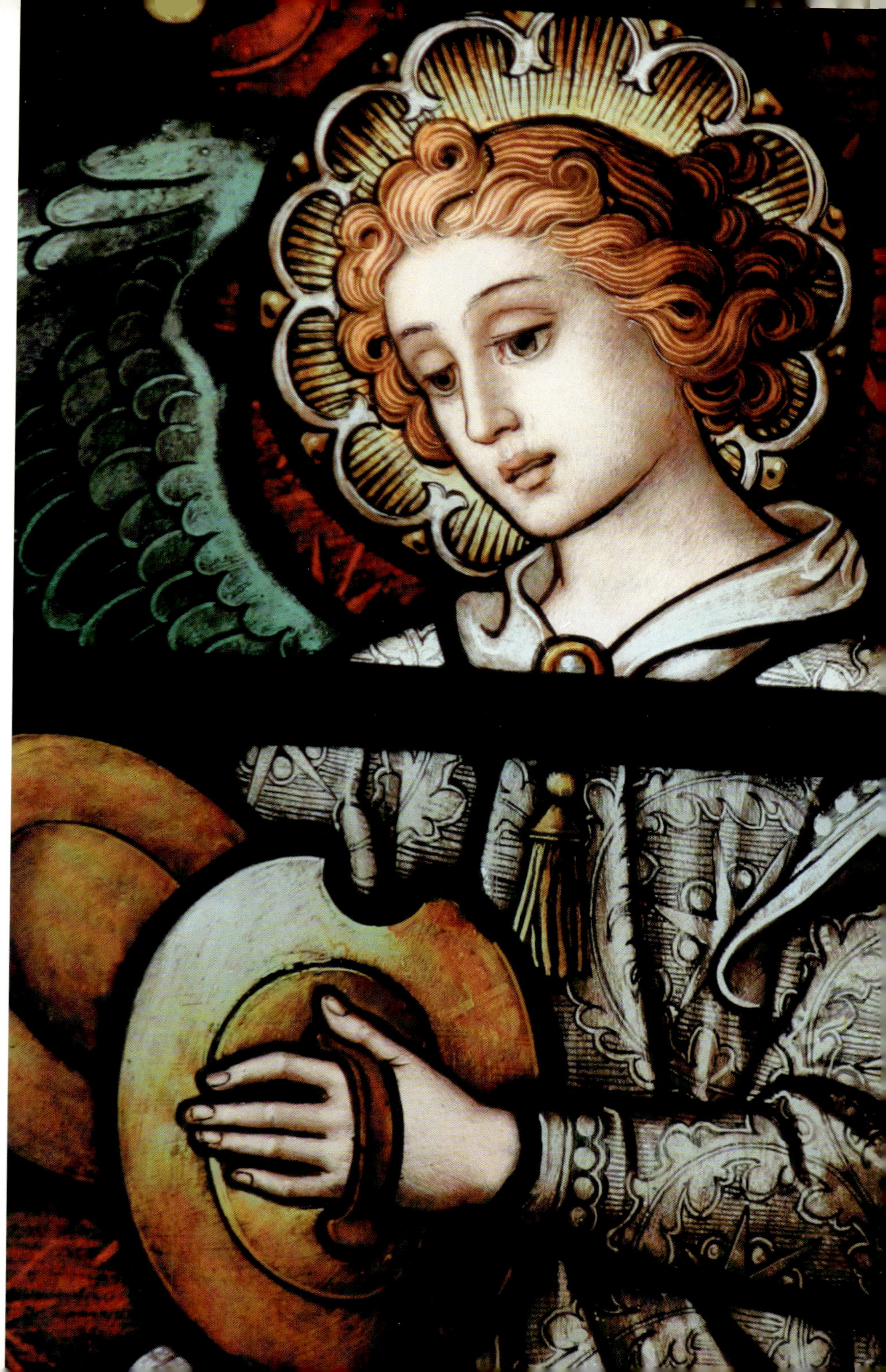

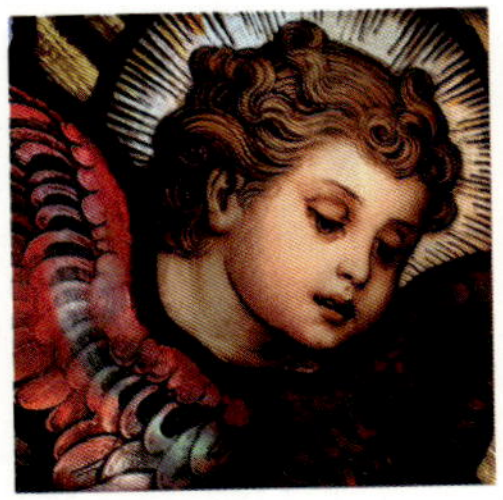

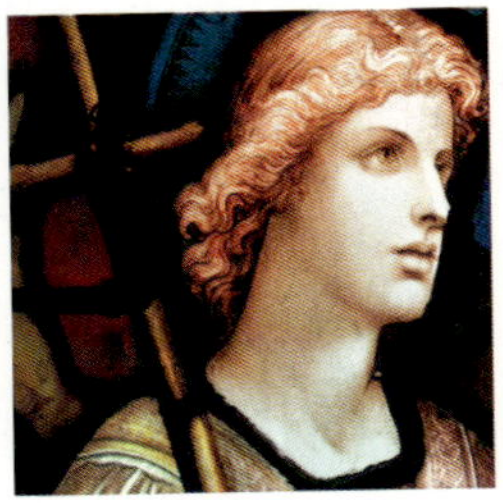

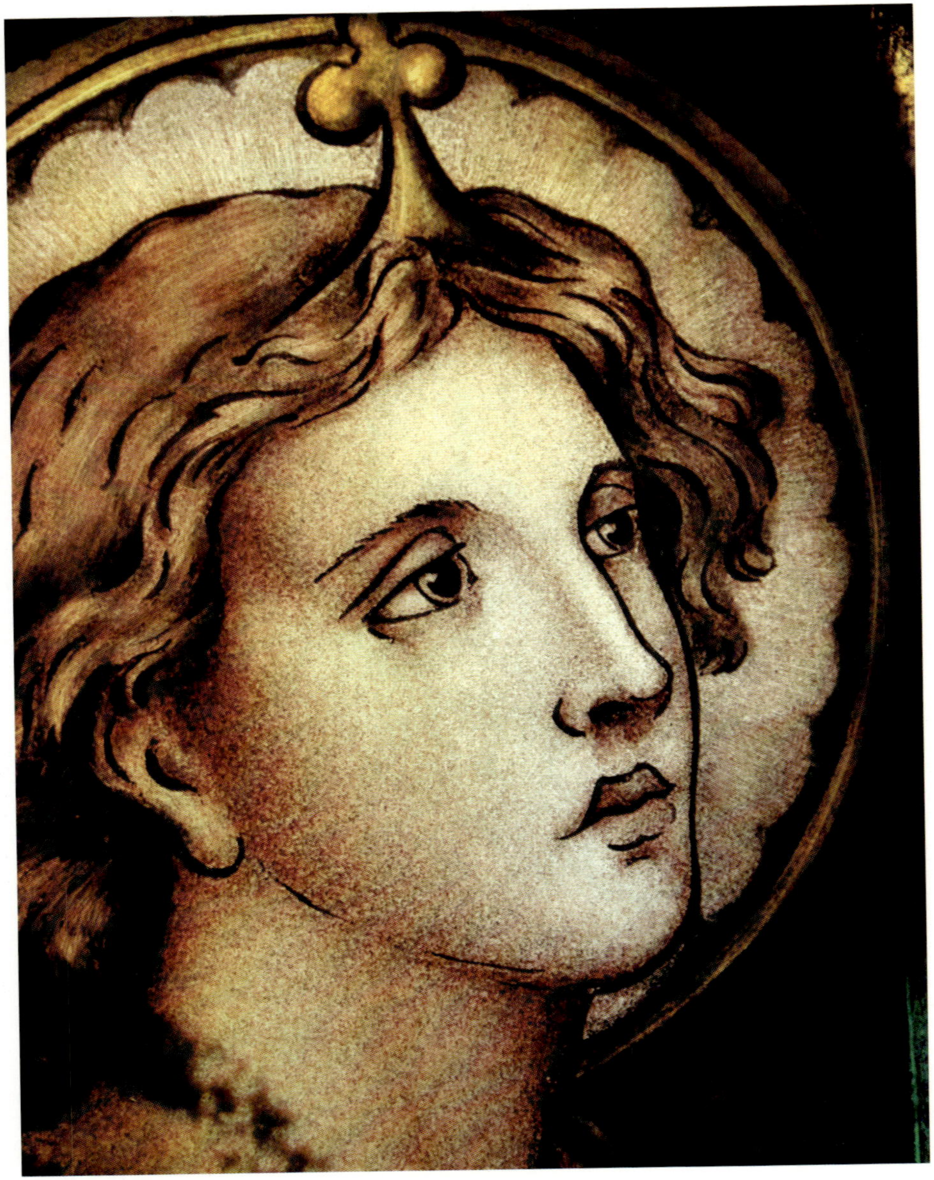

"We shall find peace. We shall hear the angels, we shall see the sky sparkling with diamonds." Anton Chekhov

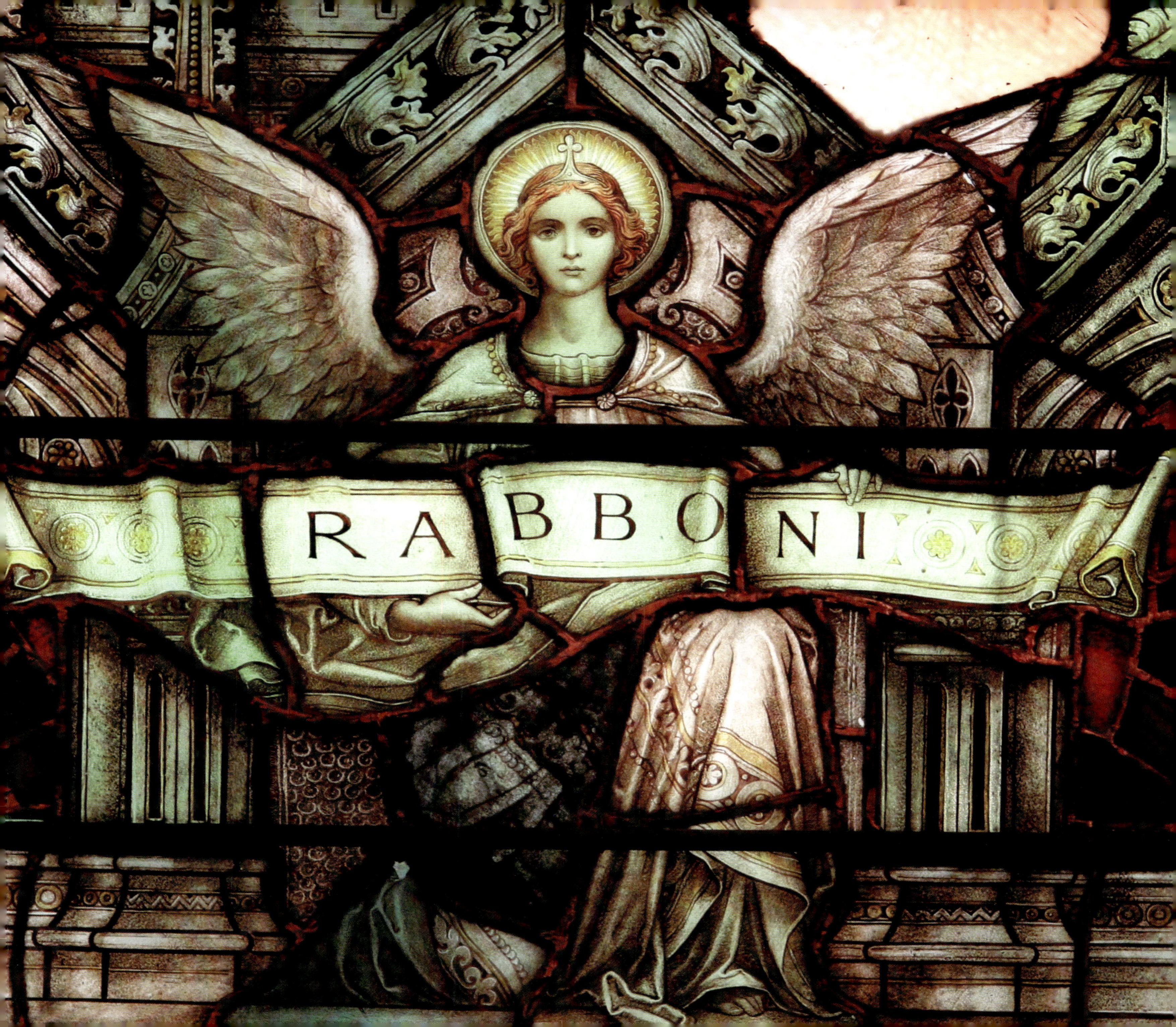
RABBONI

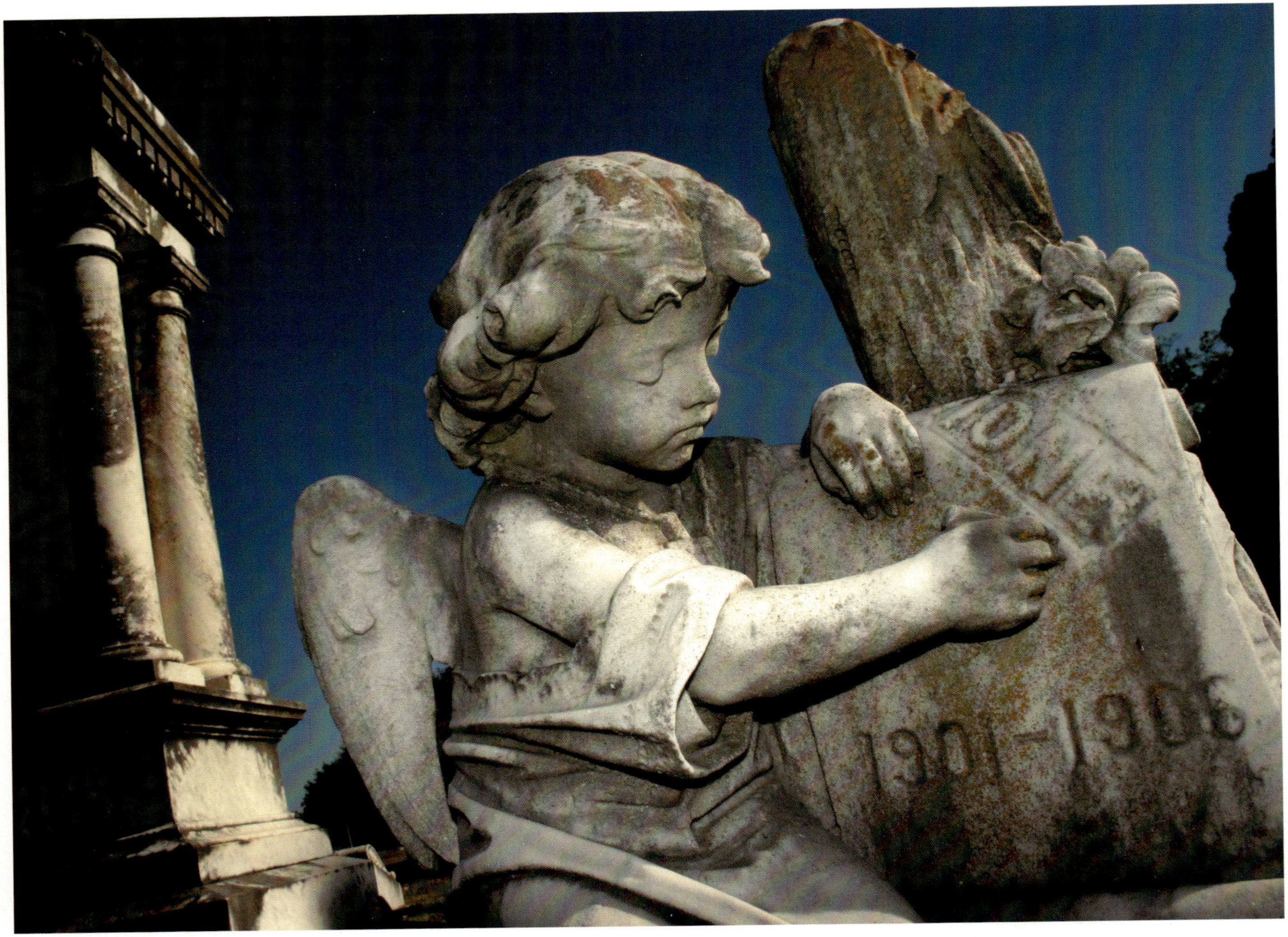

"How wonderful it would be to see angels where there are only clouds.
How sad it would be to see only clouds where there are angels."
Anonymous

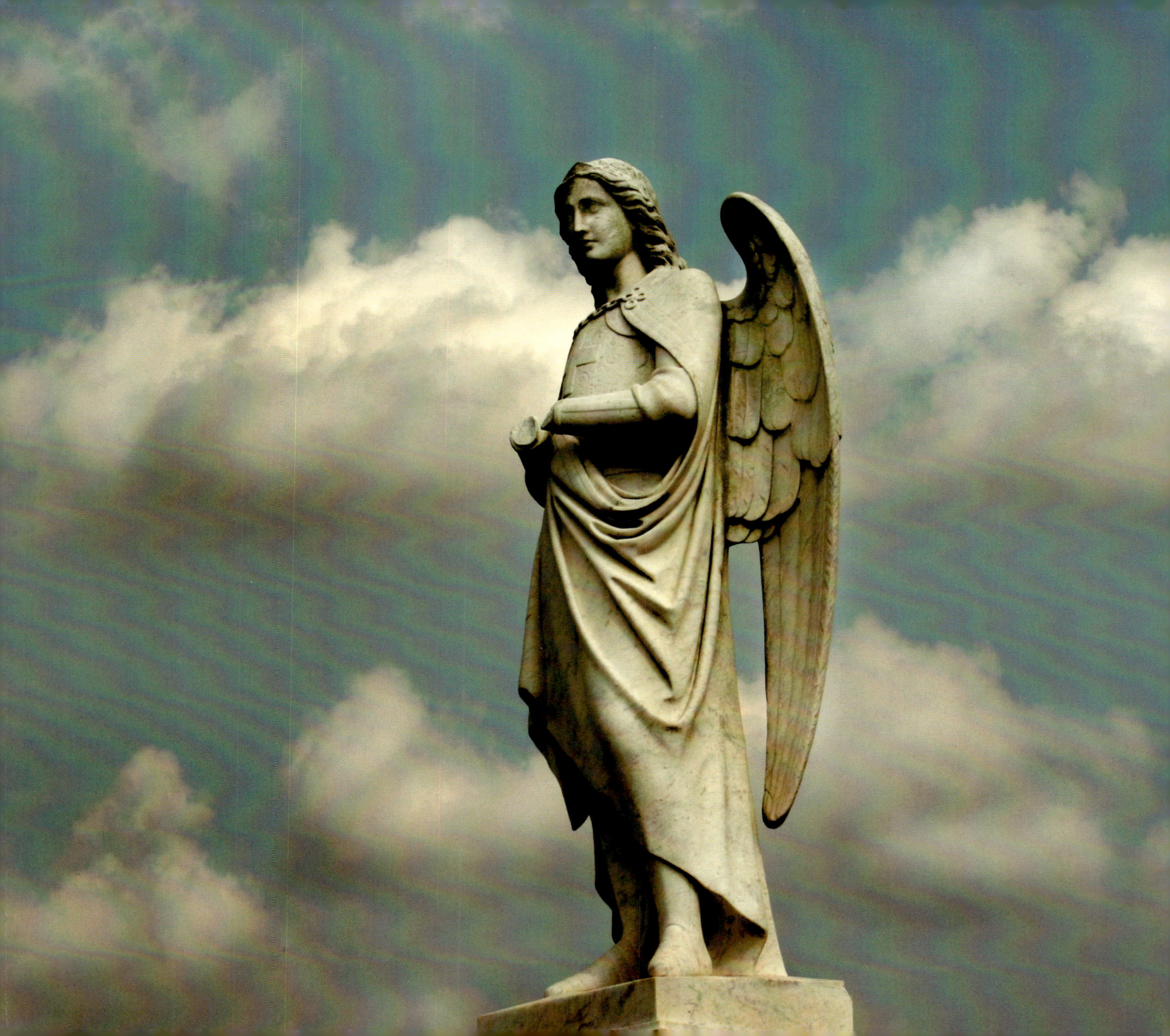

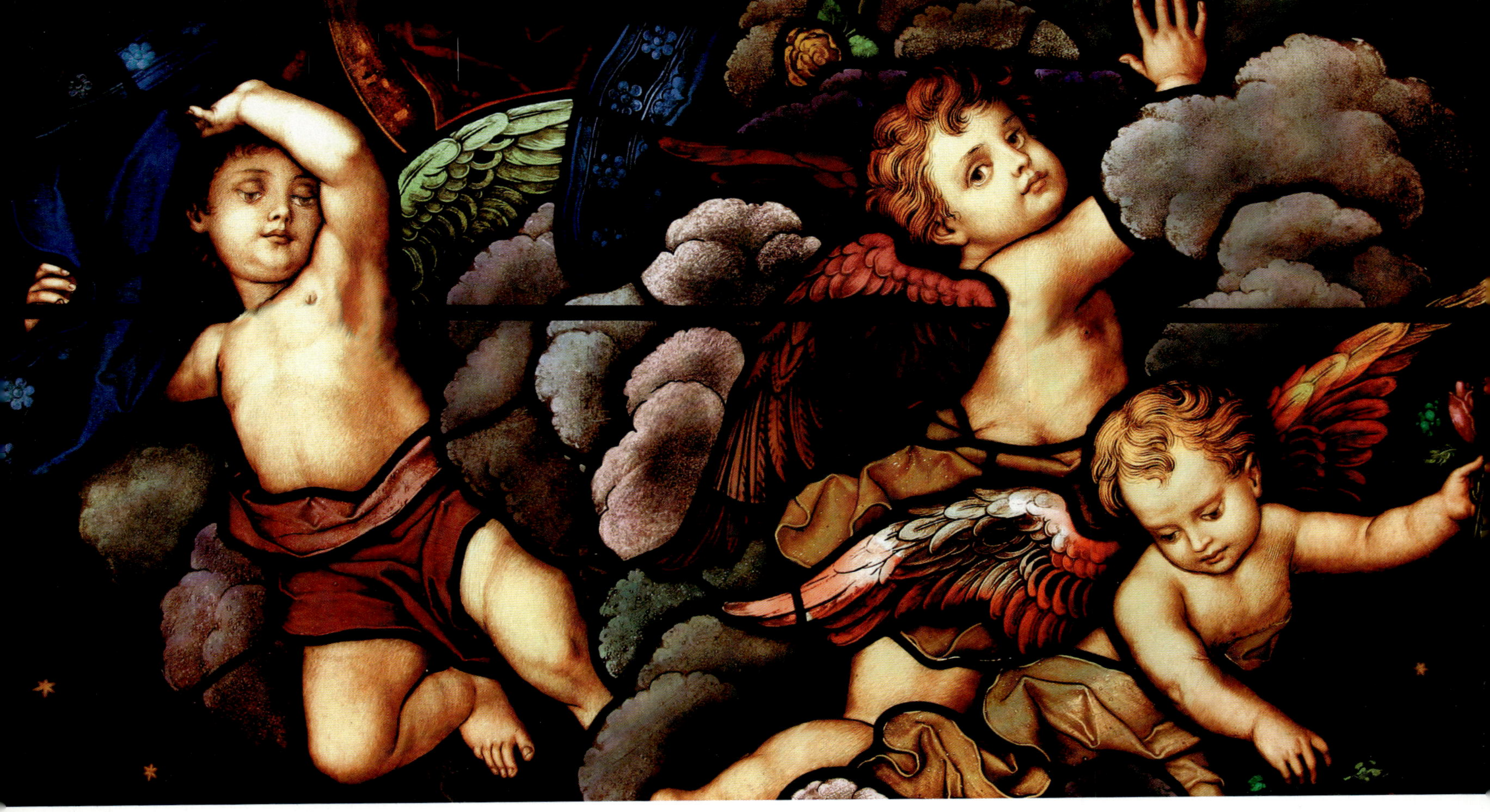

"An angel collects all the prayers
offered in the synagogues,
weaves them into garlands, and puts
them on God's head."
Anonymous

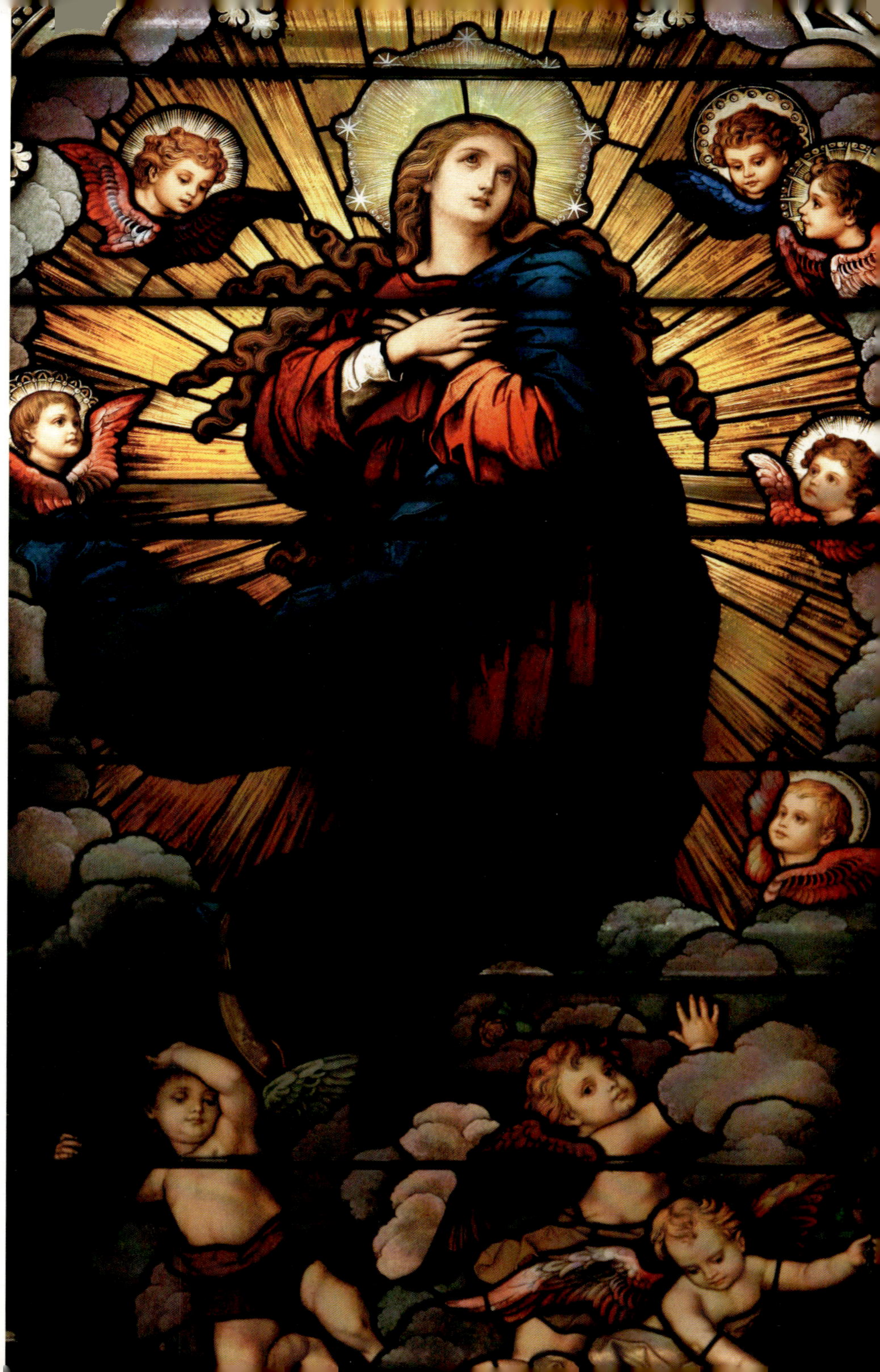

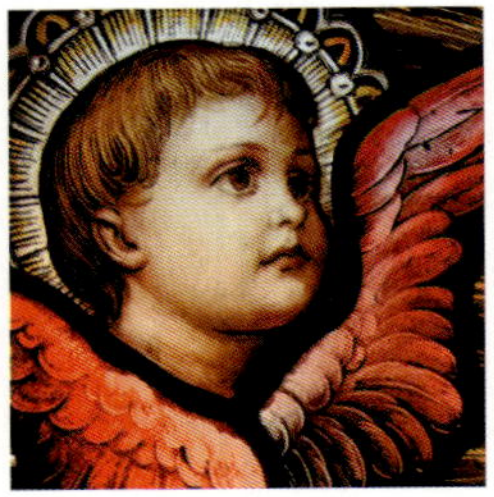

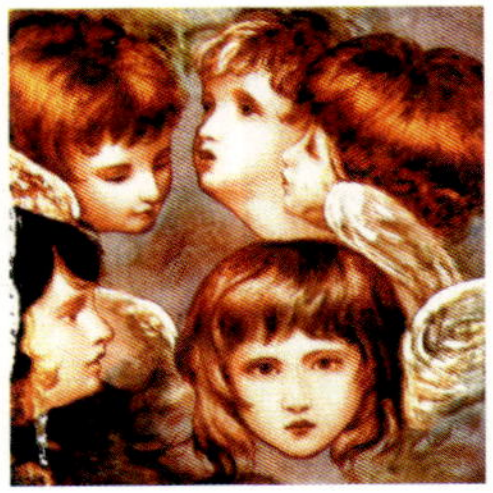

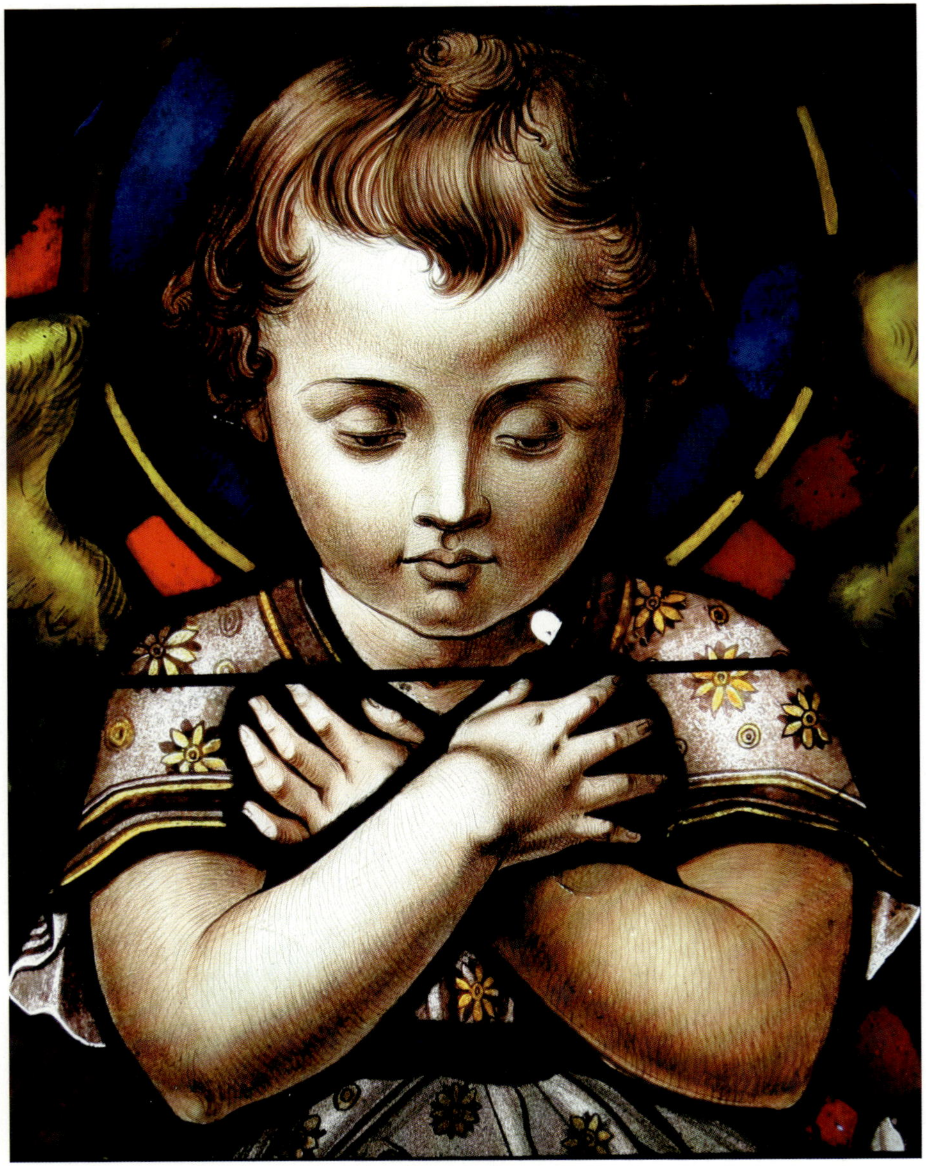

"EVERY BLADE OF GRASS HAS ITS ANGEL THAT BENDS OVER IT AND WHISPERS, 'GROW, GROW.'" THE TALMUD

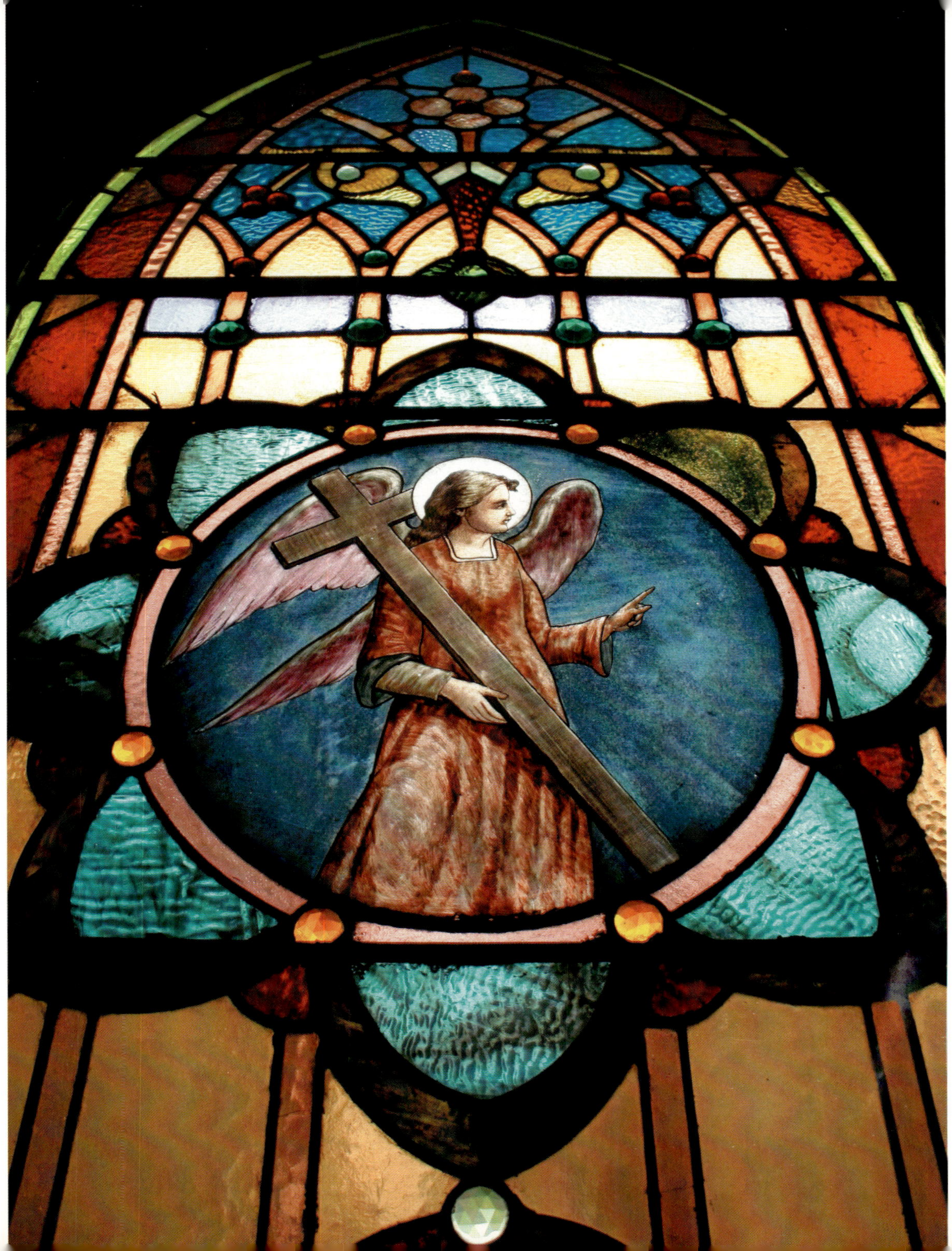

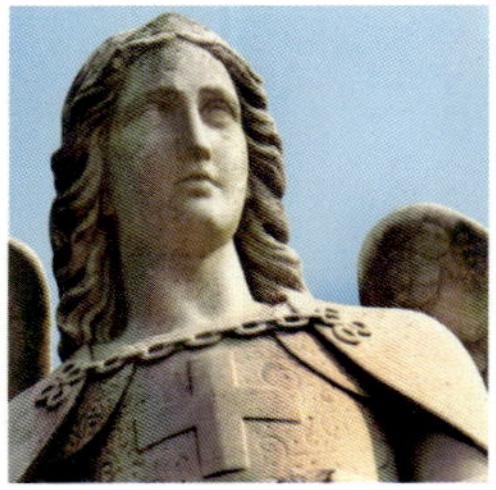

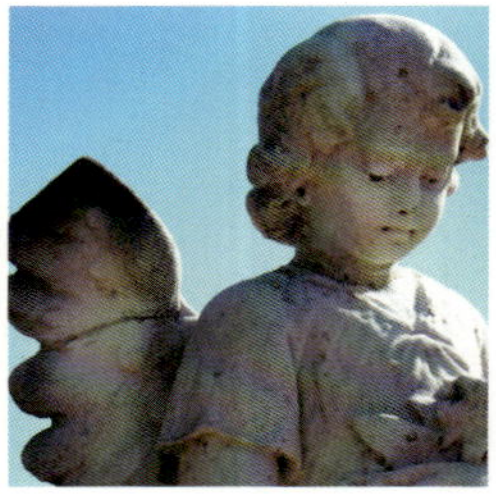

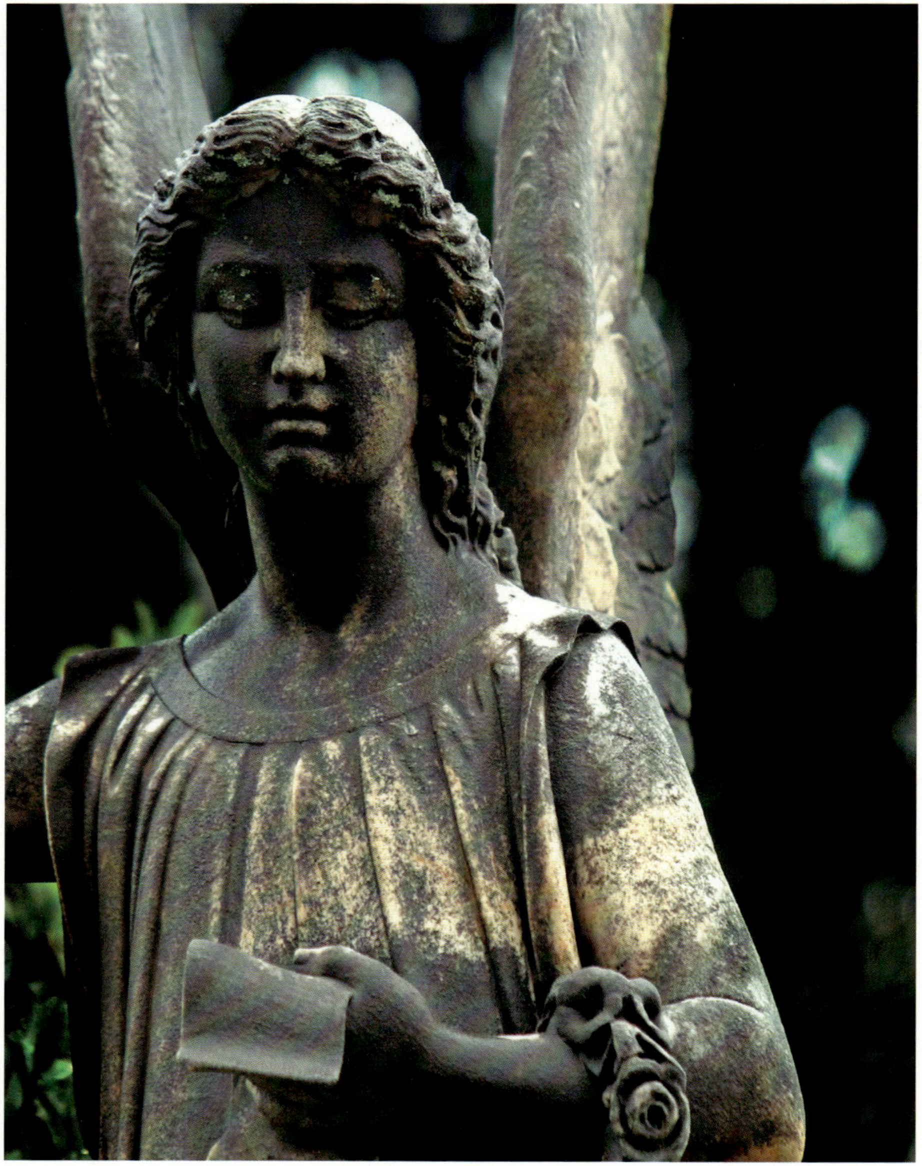

"We are never alone. Angels see our tears and cry with us.
They hear our laughter and smile." Maxie Blue

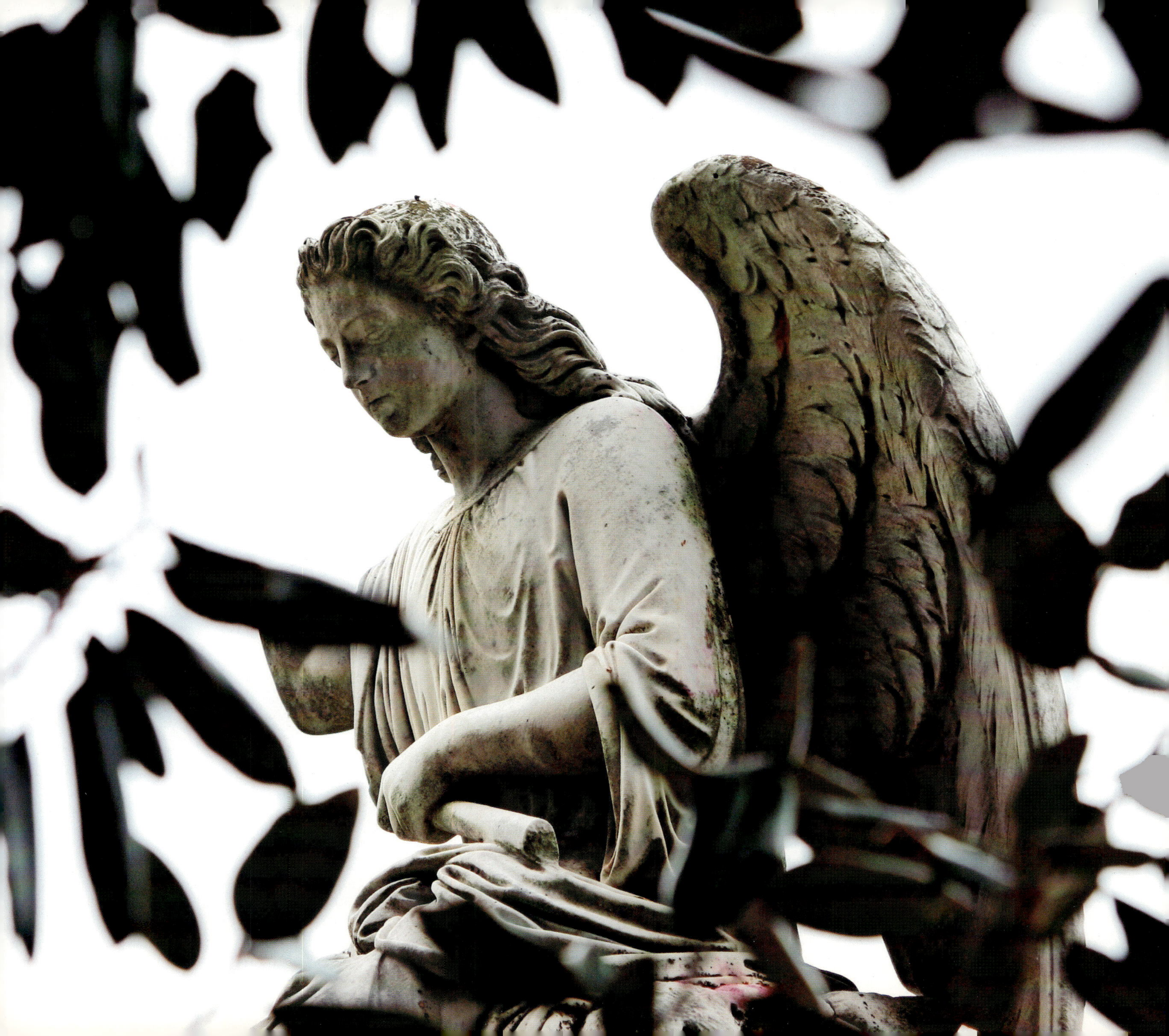

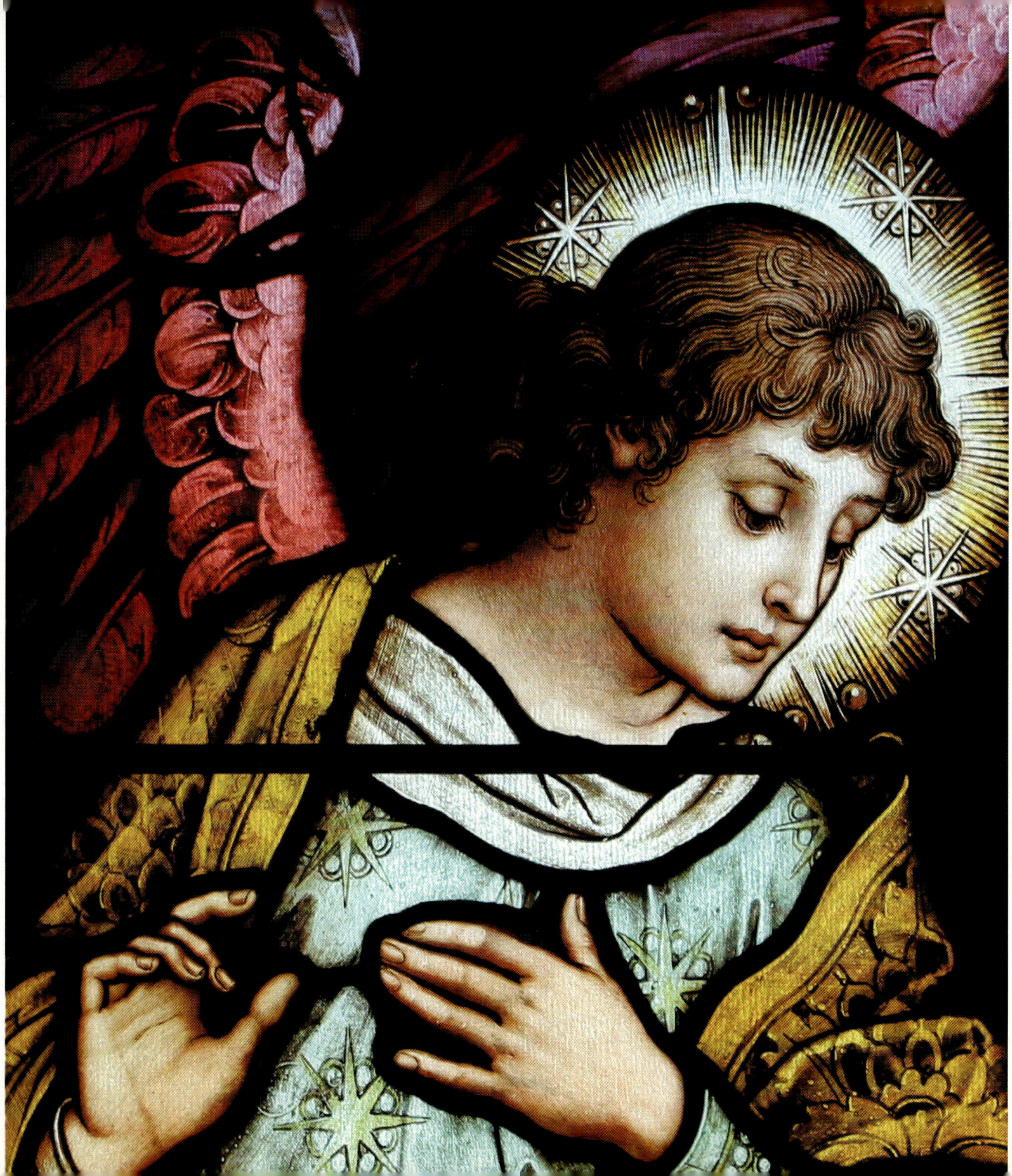

“And suddenly there was with the angel a multitude of the heavenly host, praising God and saying, Glory to God in the highest and on earth peace, good will toward men.”

Luke 2:13-14

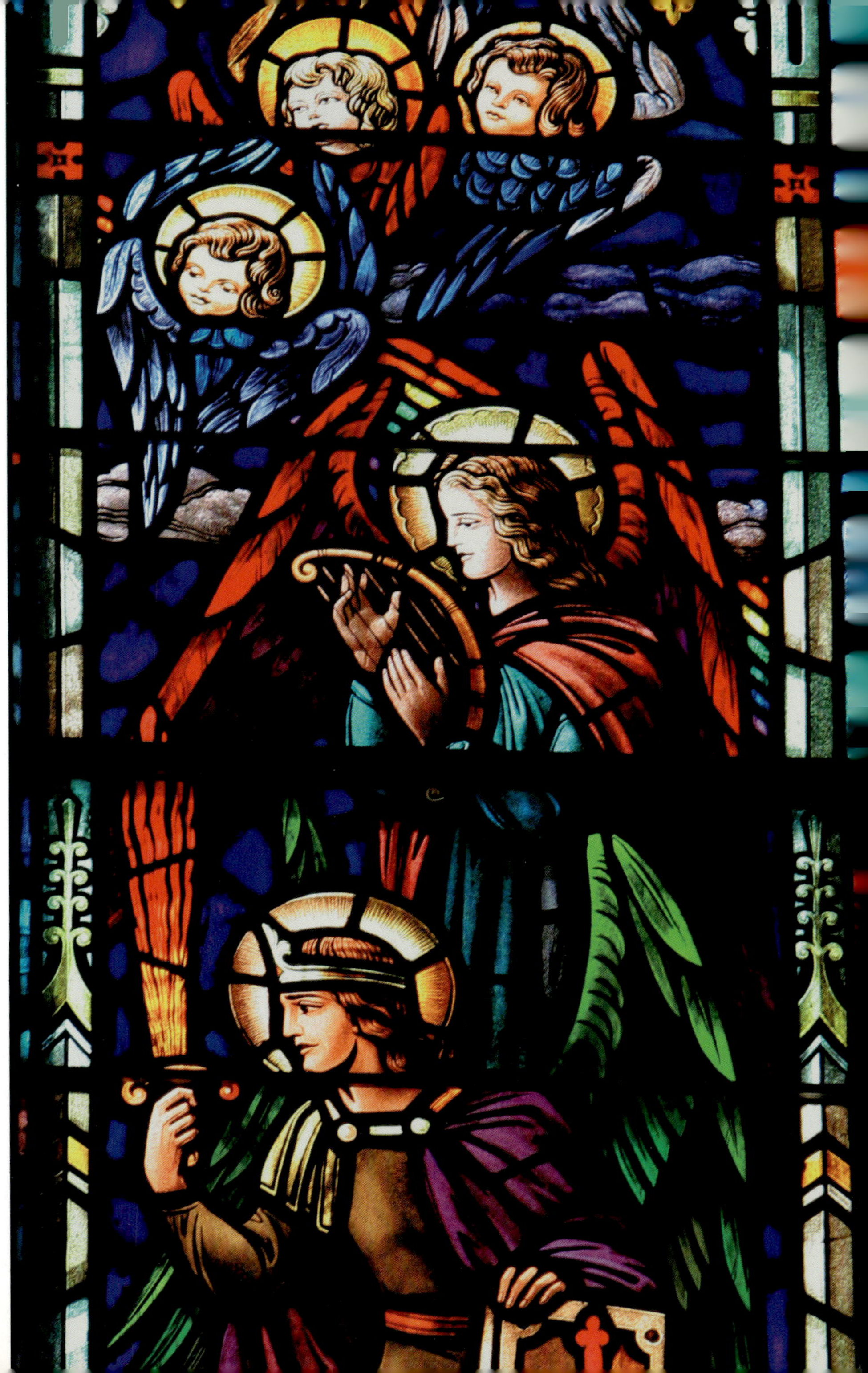

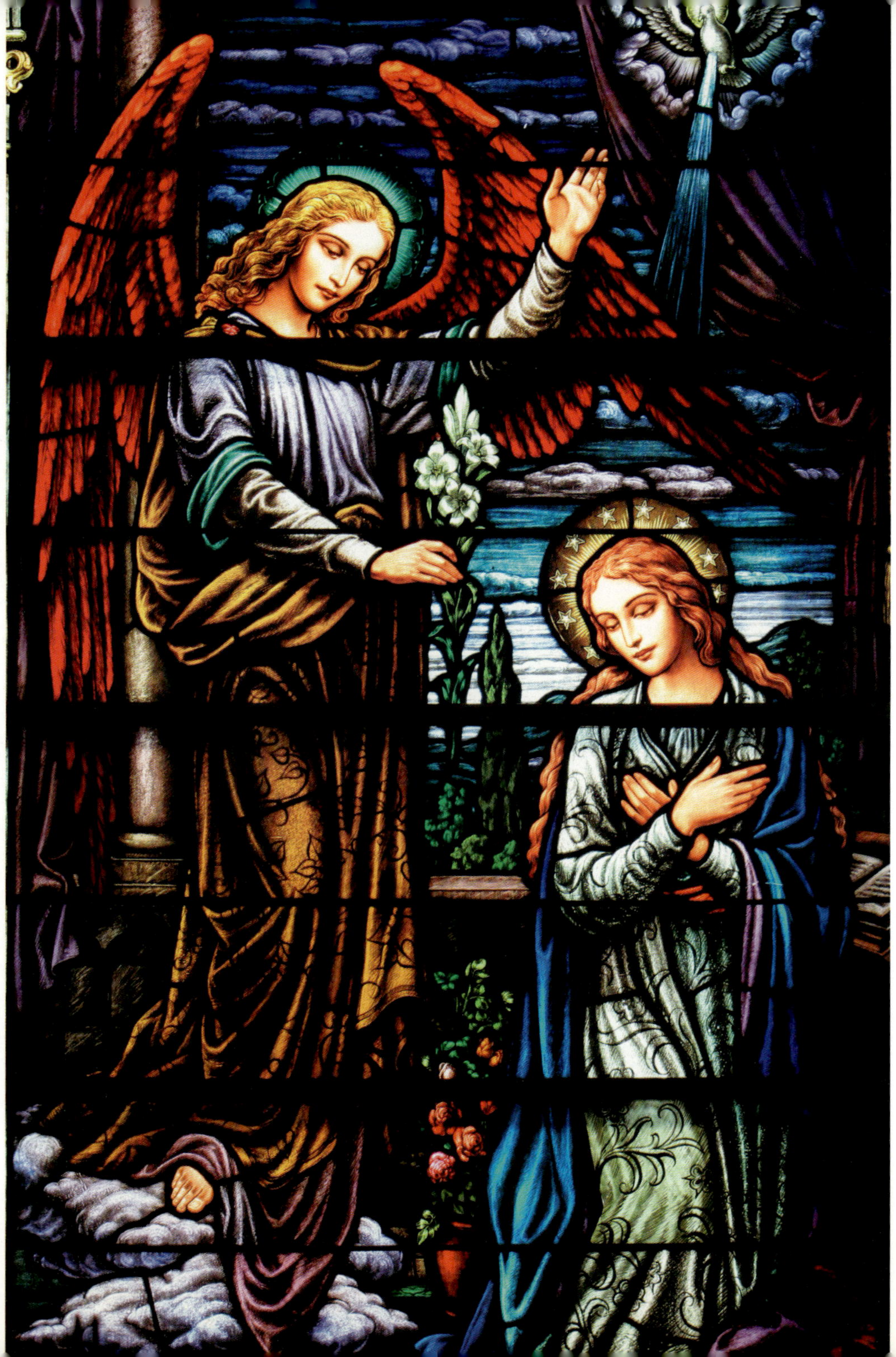

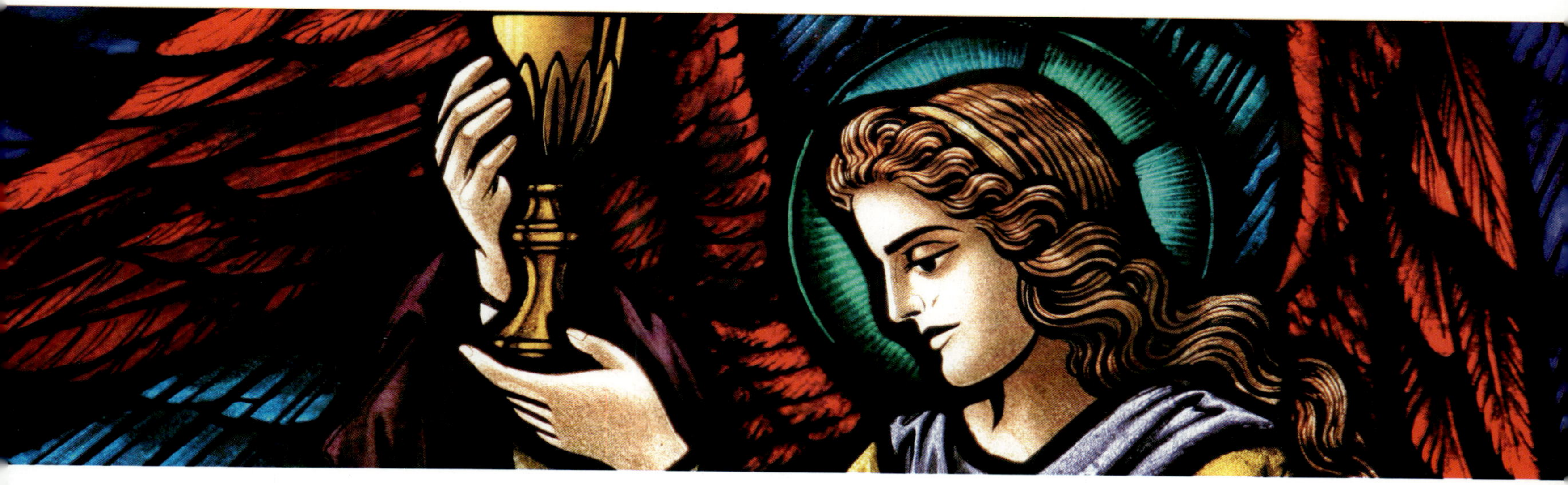

"The golden moments in the stream of life rush past us and we see nothing but sand; the angels come to visit us, and we only know them when they are gone."
George Eliot

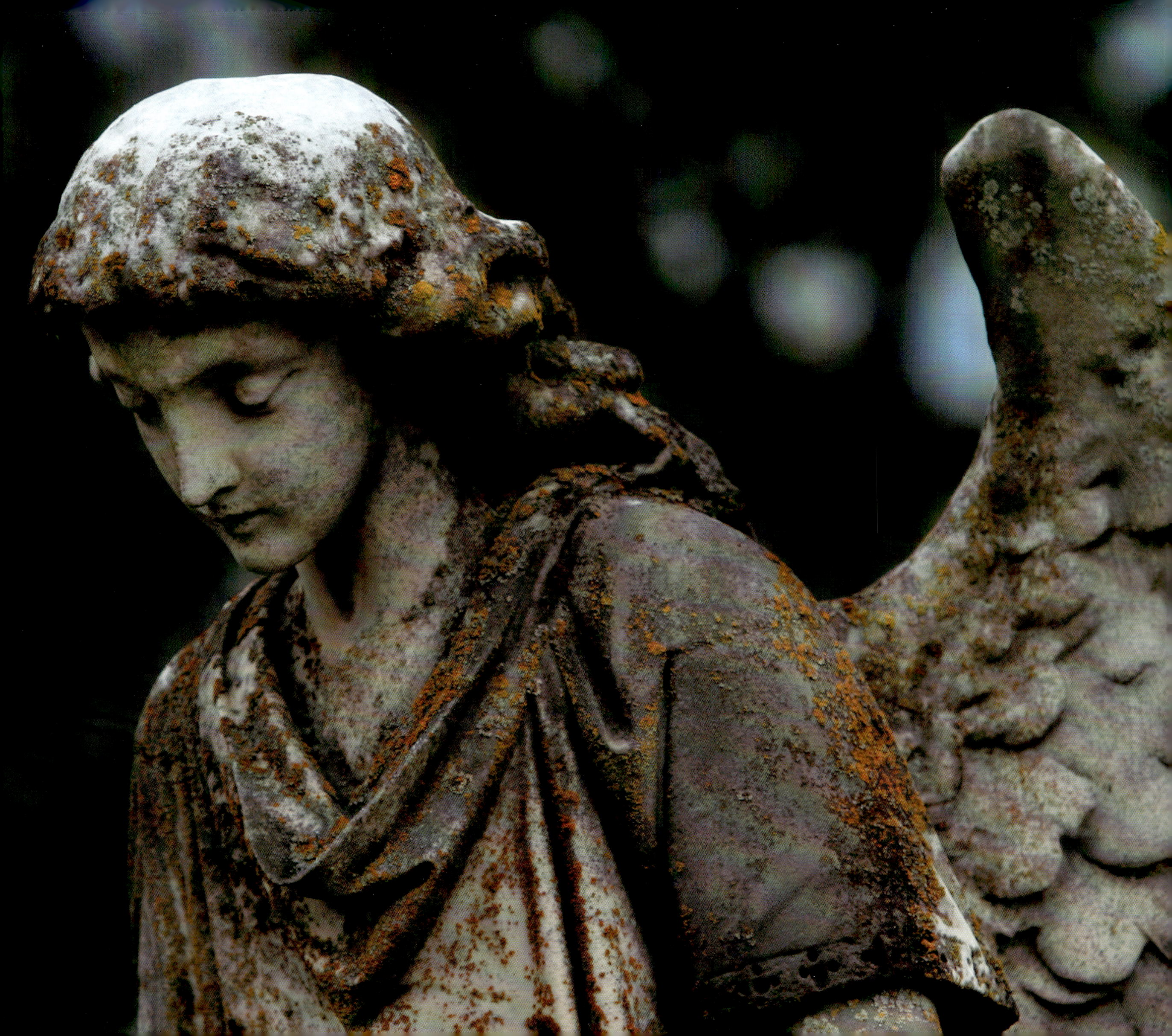

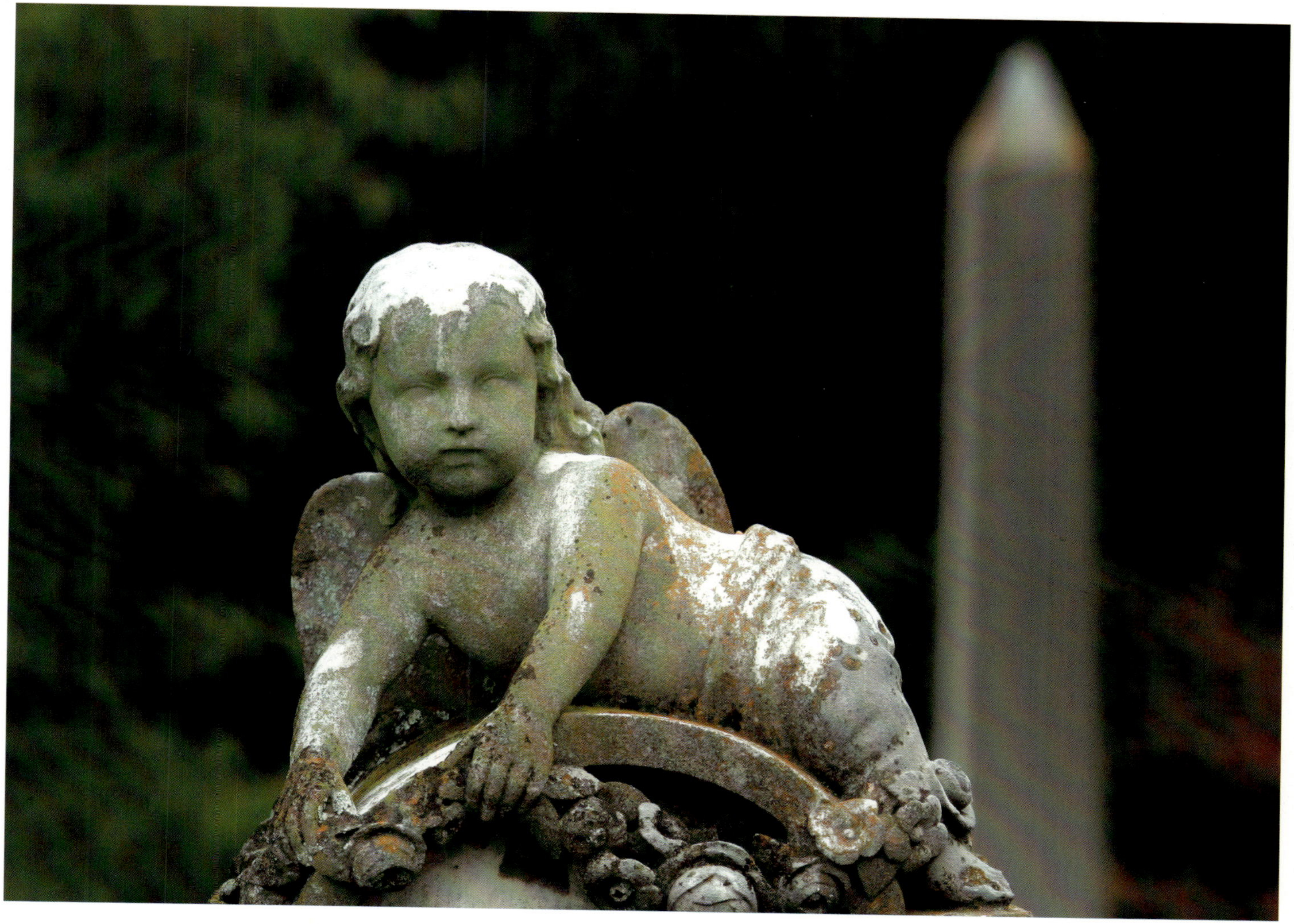

"An angel doesn't have to be physical to touch you."
Anonymous

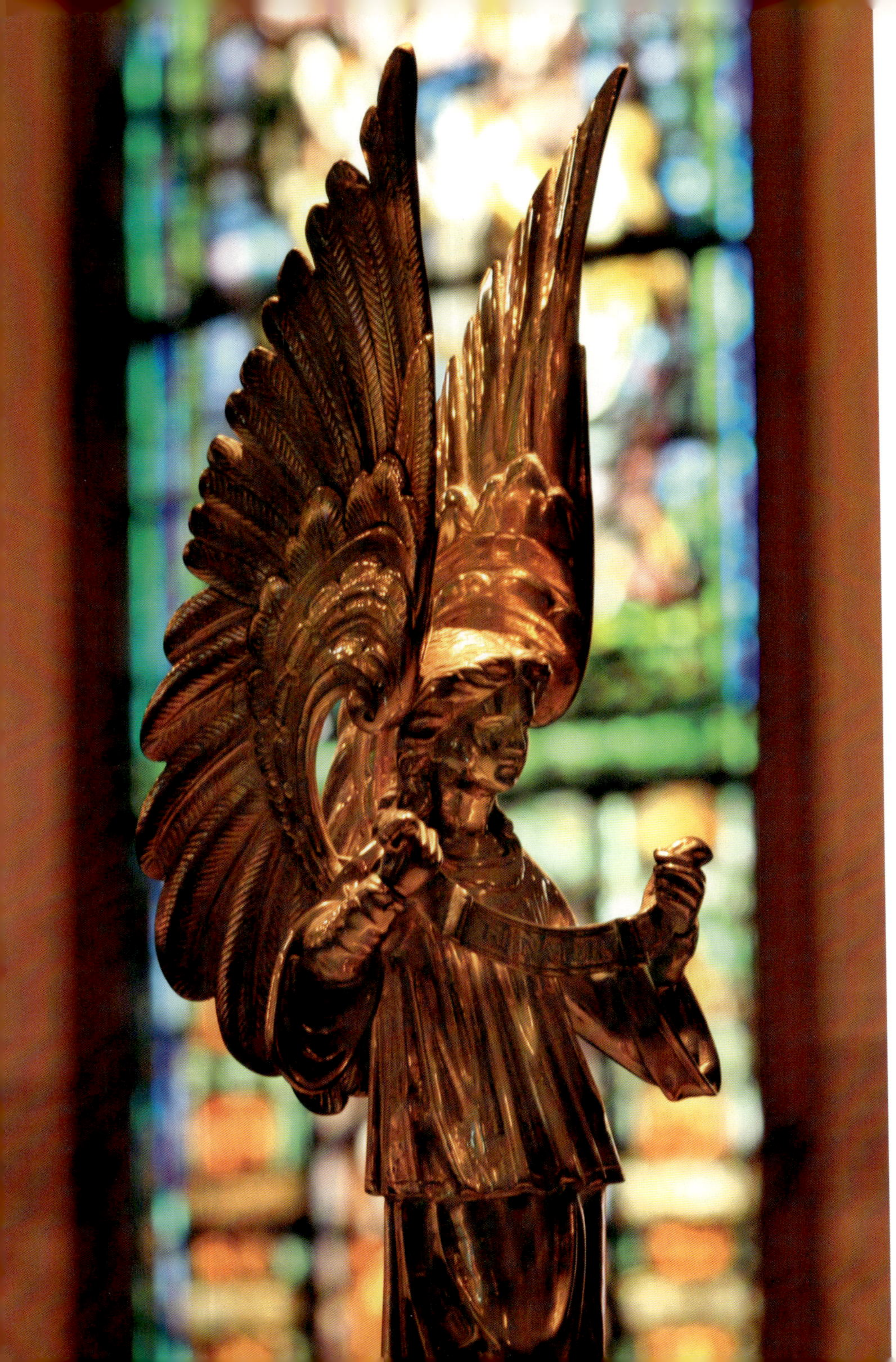

"Make yourself familiar with
the angels and behold them
frequently in spirit;
for without being seen,
they are present with you."

St. Francis de Sales

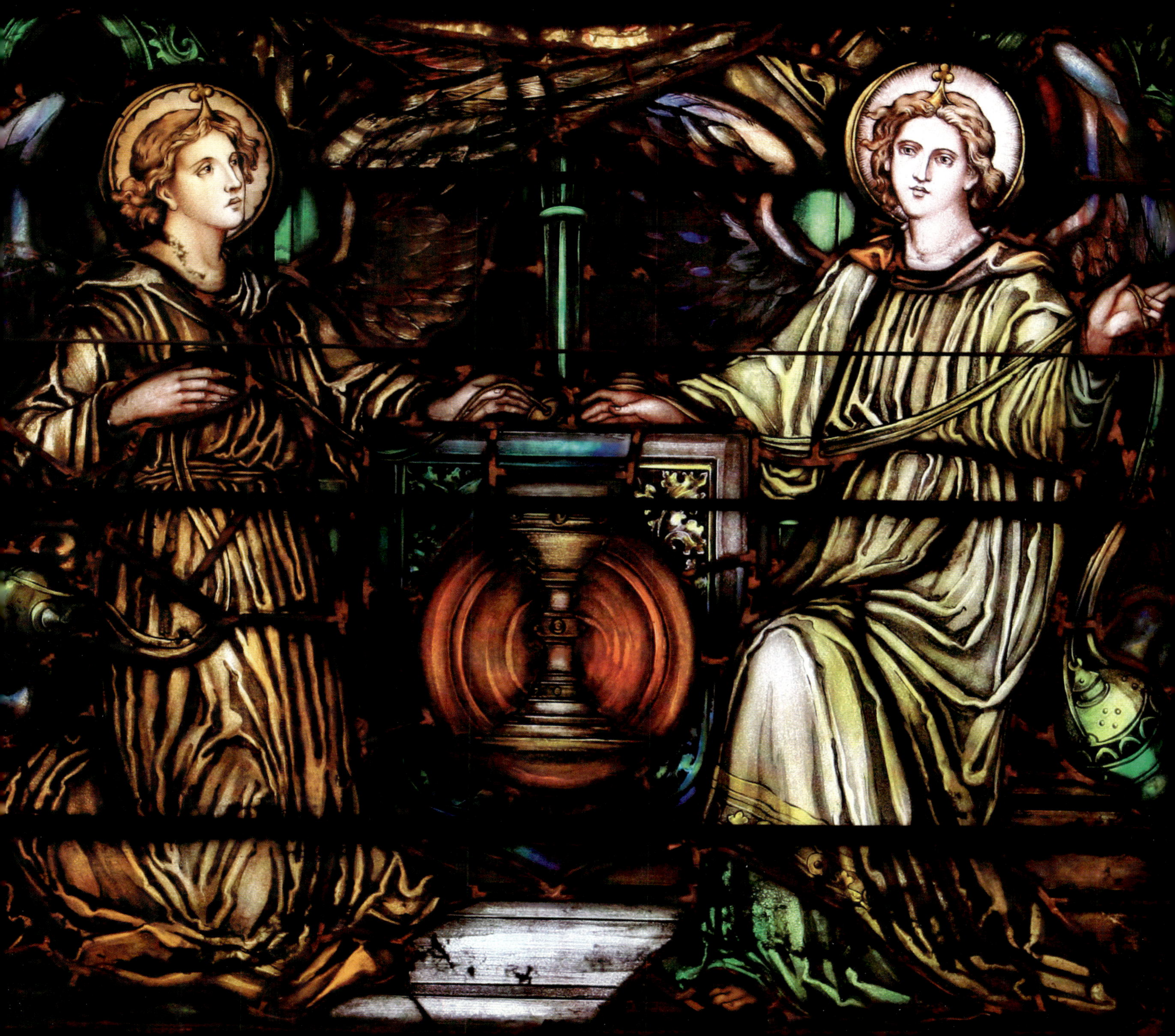

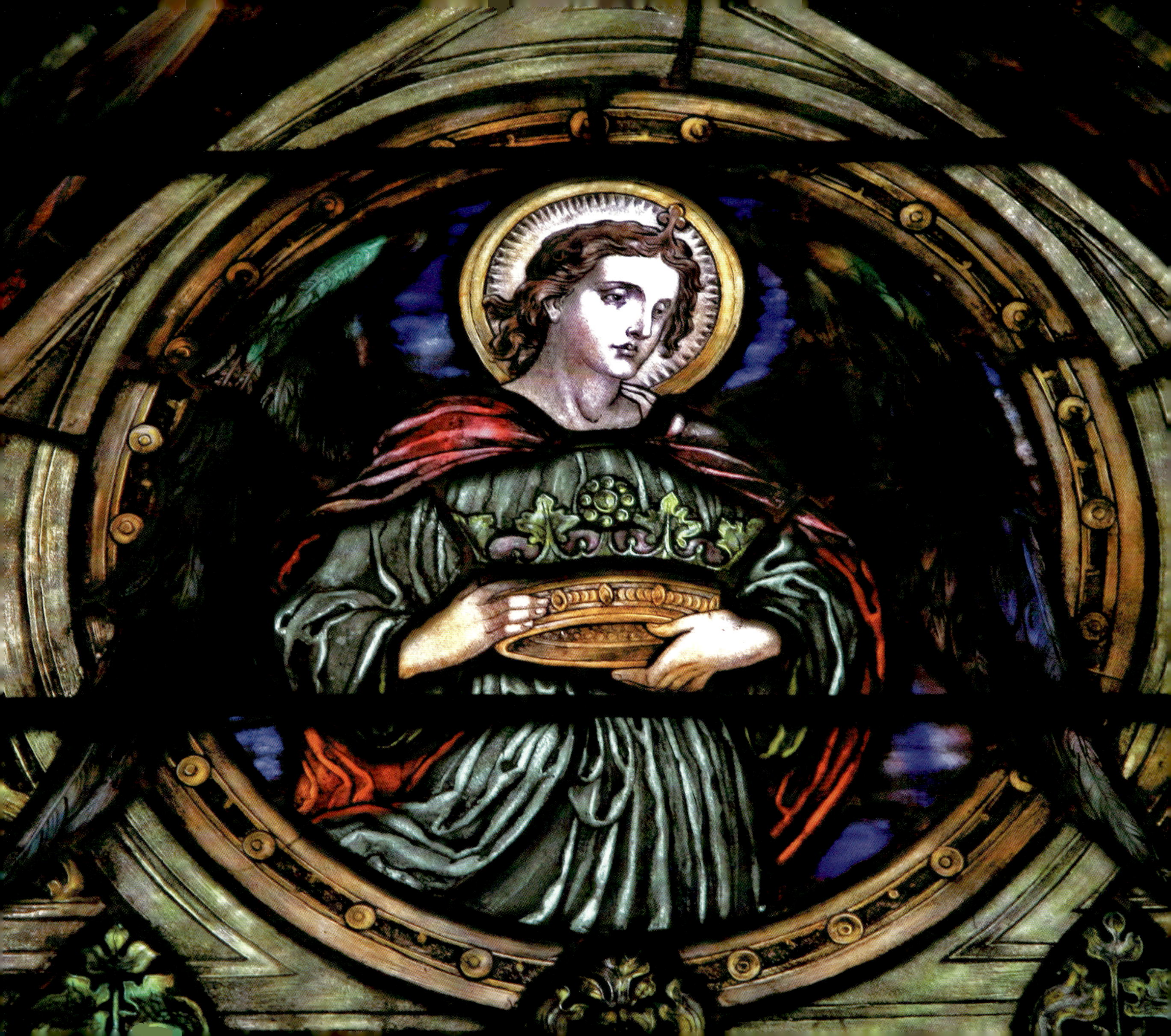

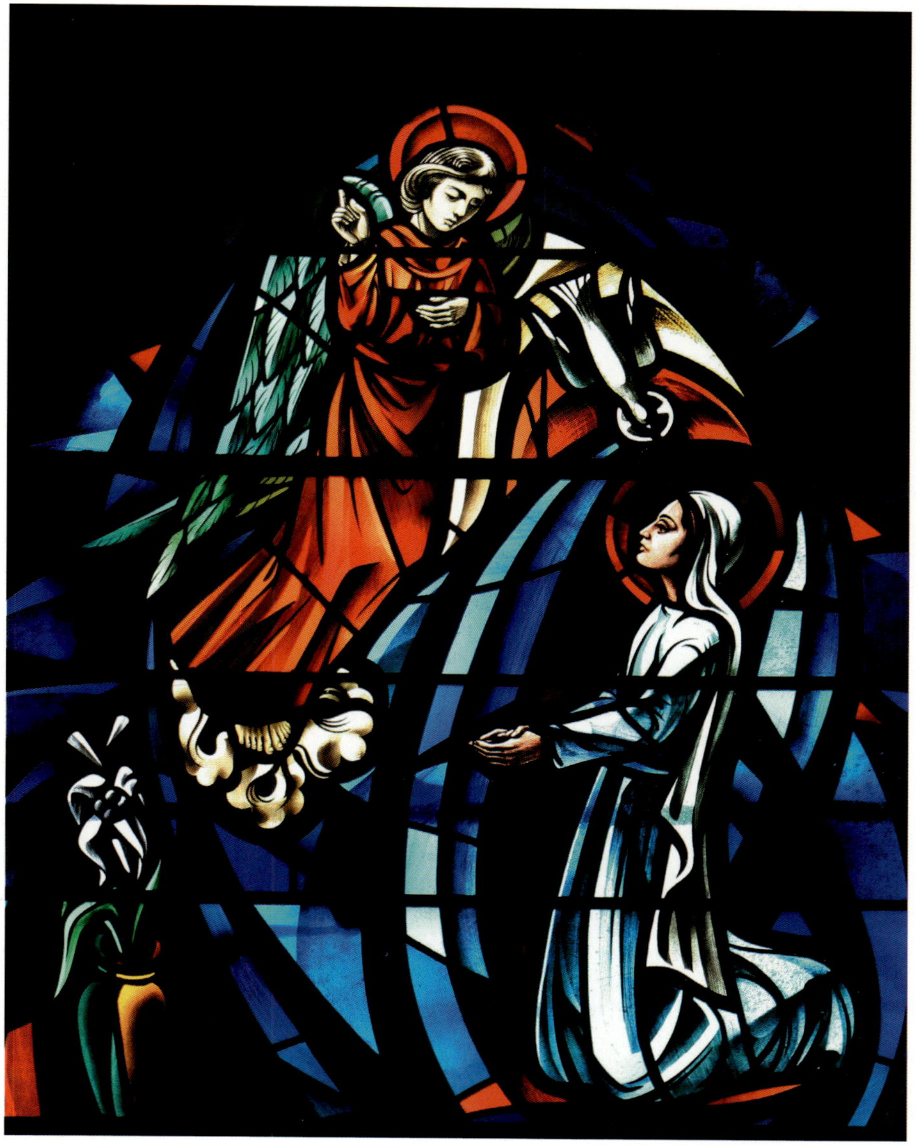

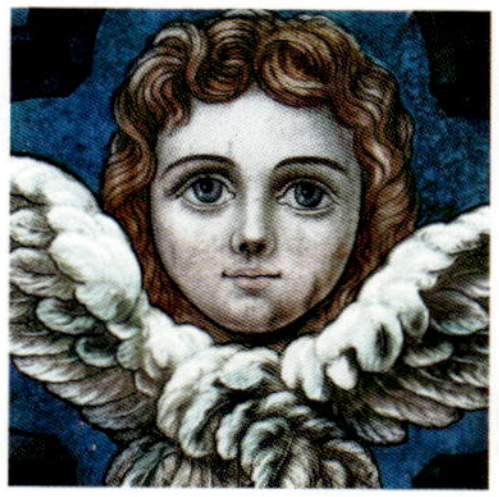

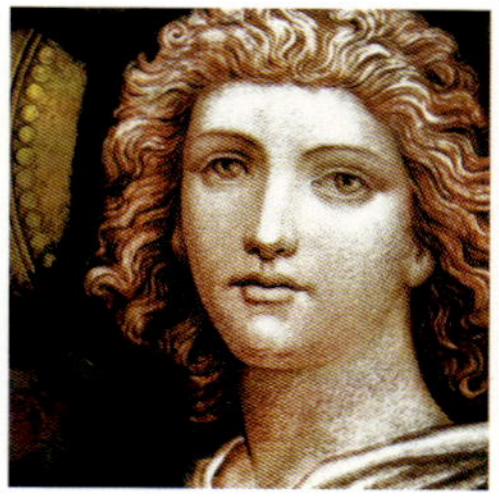

"Angels descending, bring from above,
Echoes of mercy, whispers of love."
Fanny J. Crosby

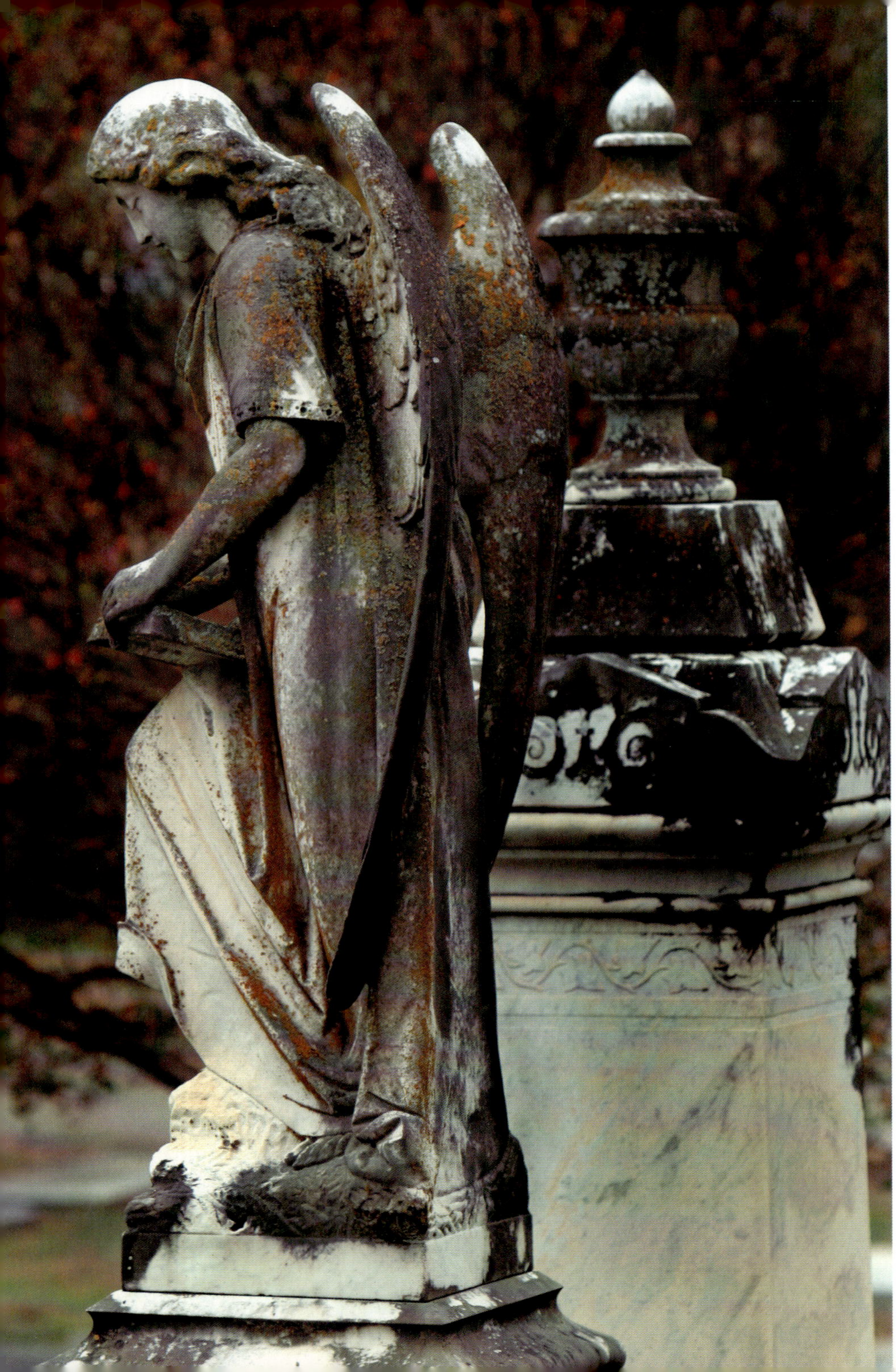

"In the darkest hour when my
heart was shattered and I felt
I could not go on;
I felt the presence of an angel.
In the warmth of the angel's wings
around my shoulders;
I found peace.
In the saltiness of the angel's tears
mingled with my own;
I found comfort.
In the kiss of the angel's lips
upon my brow;
I found hope."

Michal Bradley

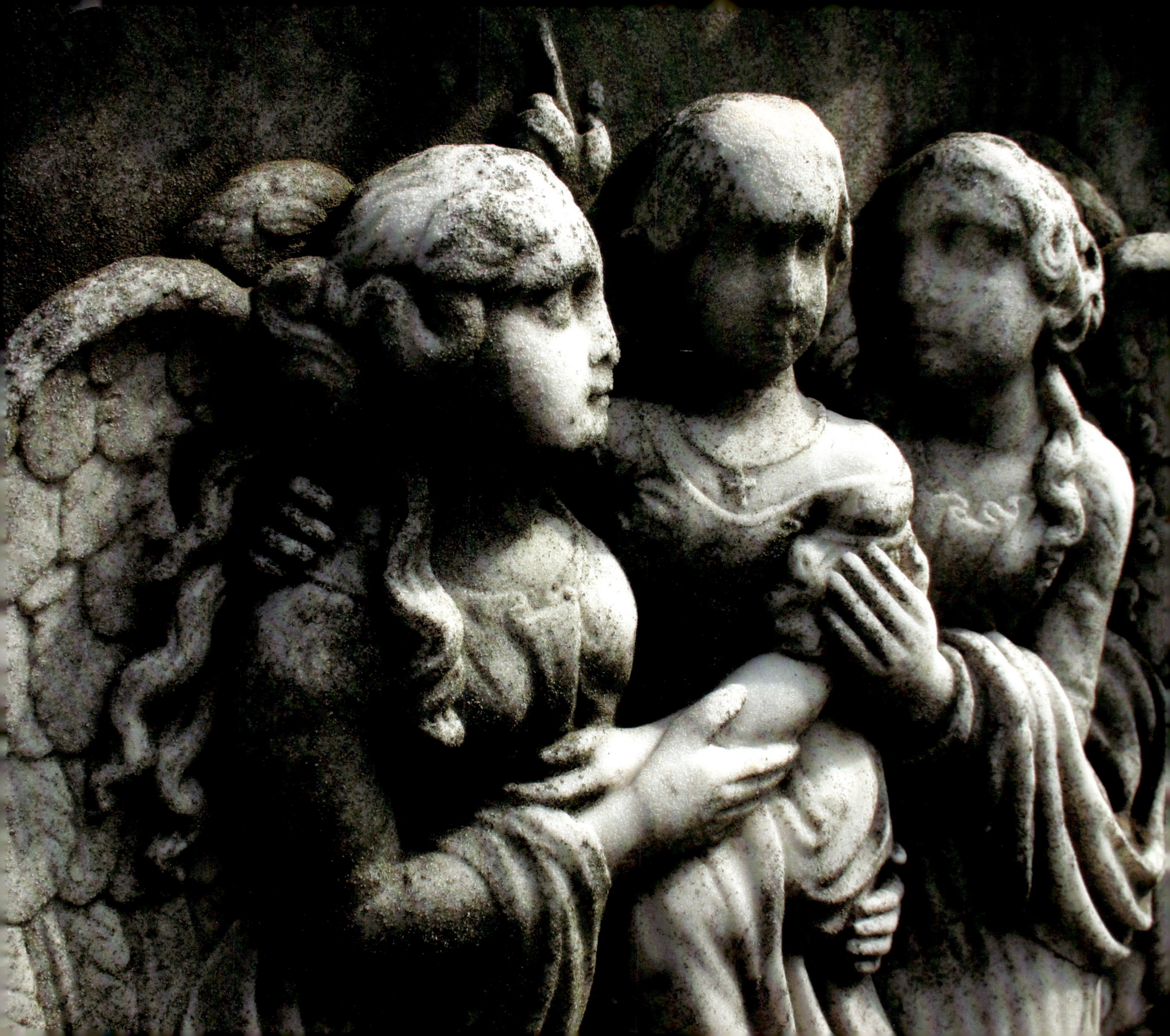

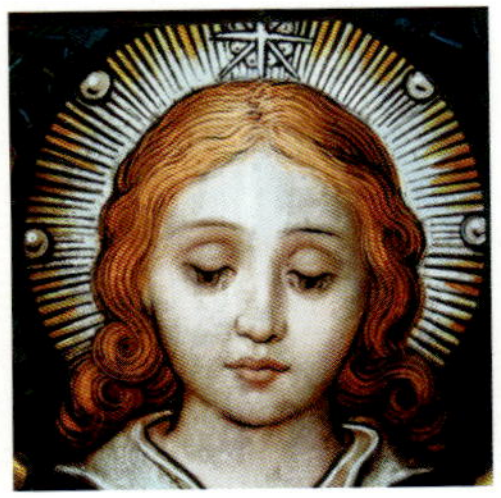

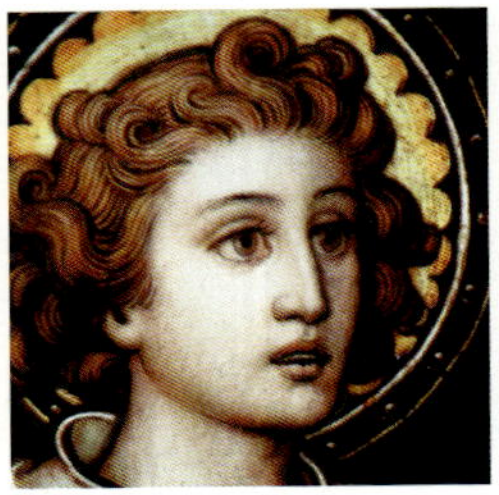

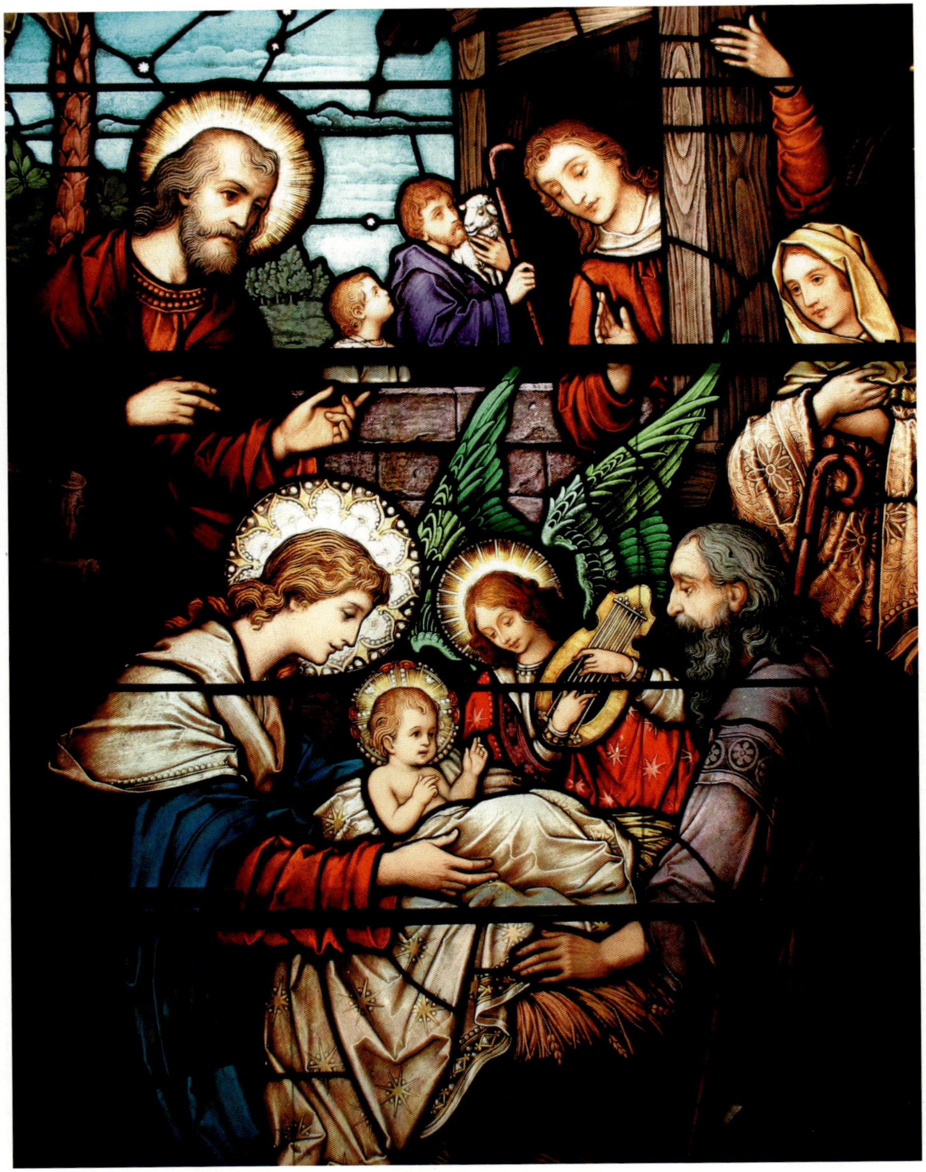

"HARK! THE HERALD ANGELS SING,
GLORY TO THE NEWBORN KING."

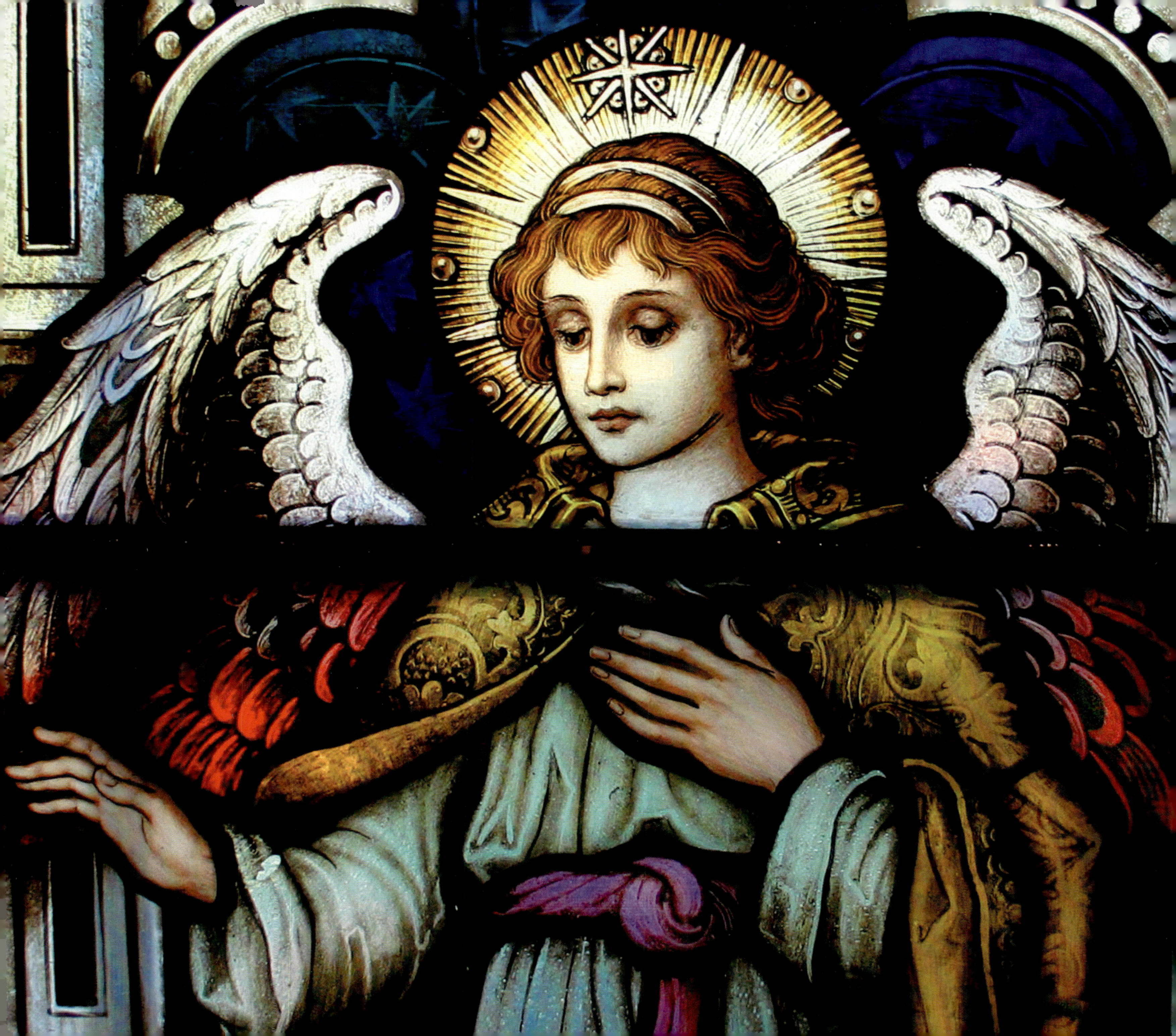

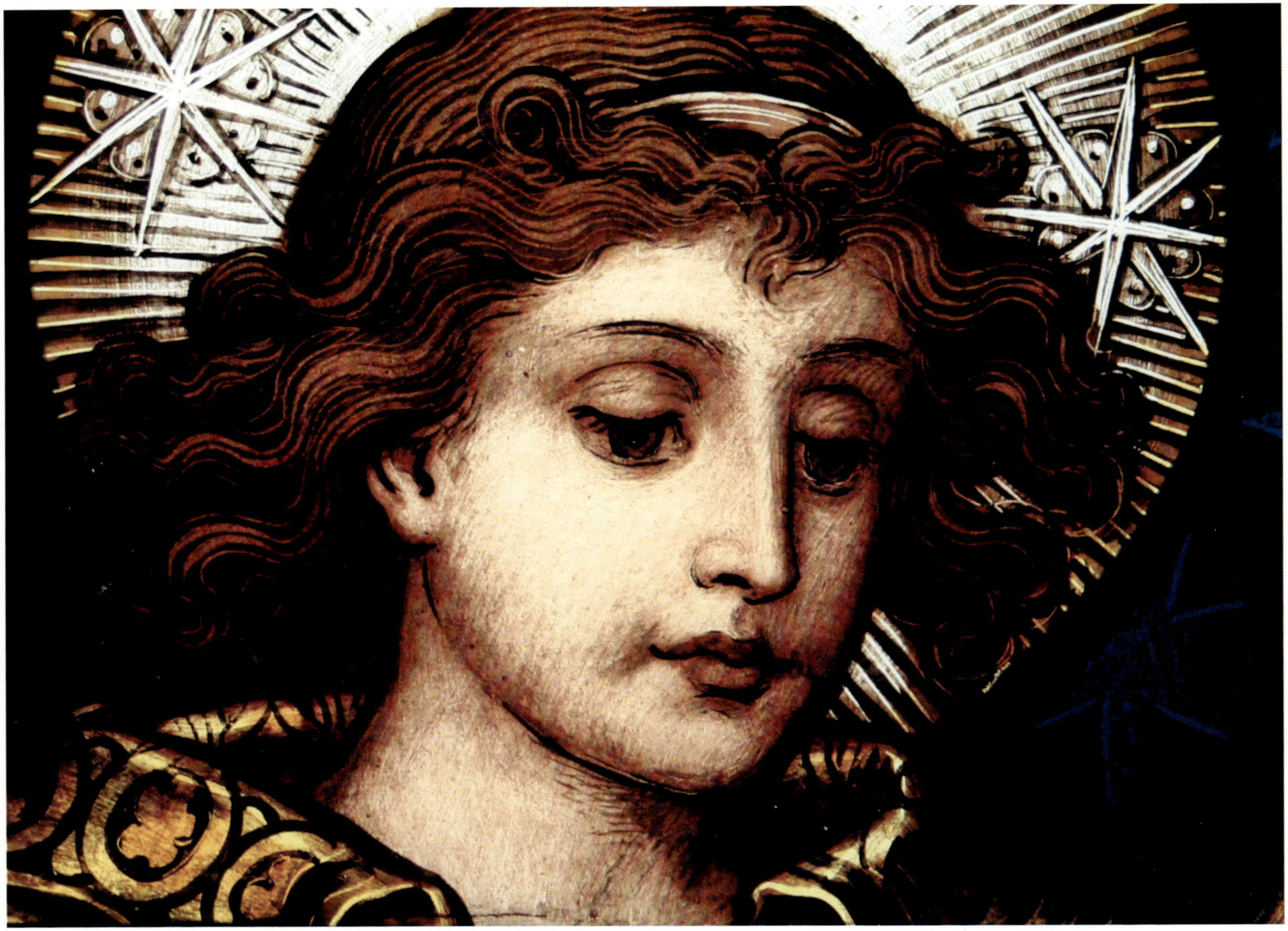

"ANGELS DREAM BEAUTIFUL VISIONS OF THE WORLD."
ANONYMOUS

"If we could perceive our angels for just a single day, this world would never be the same again. Nor would it ever wish to be."

Anonymous

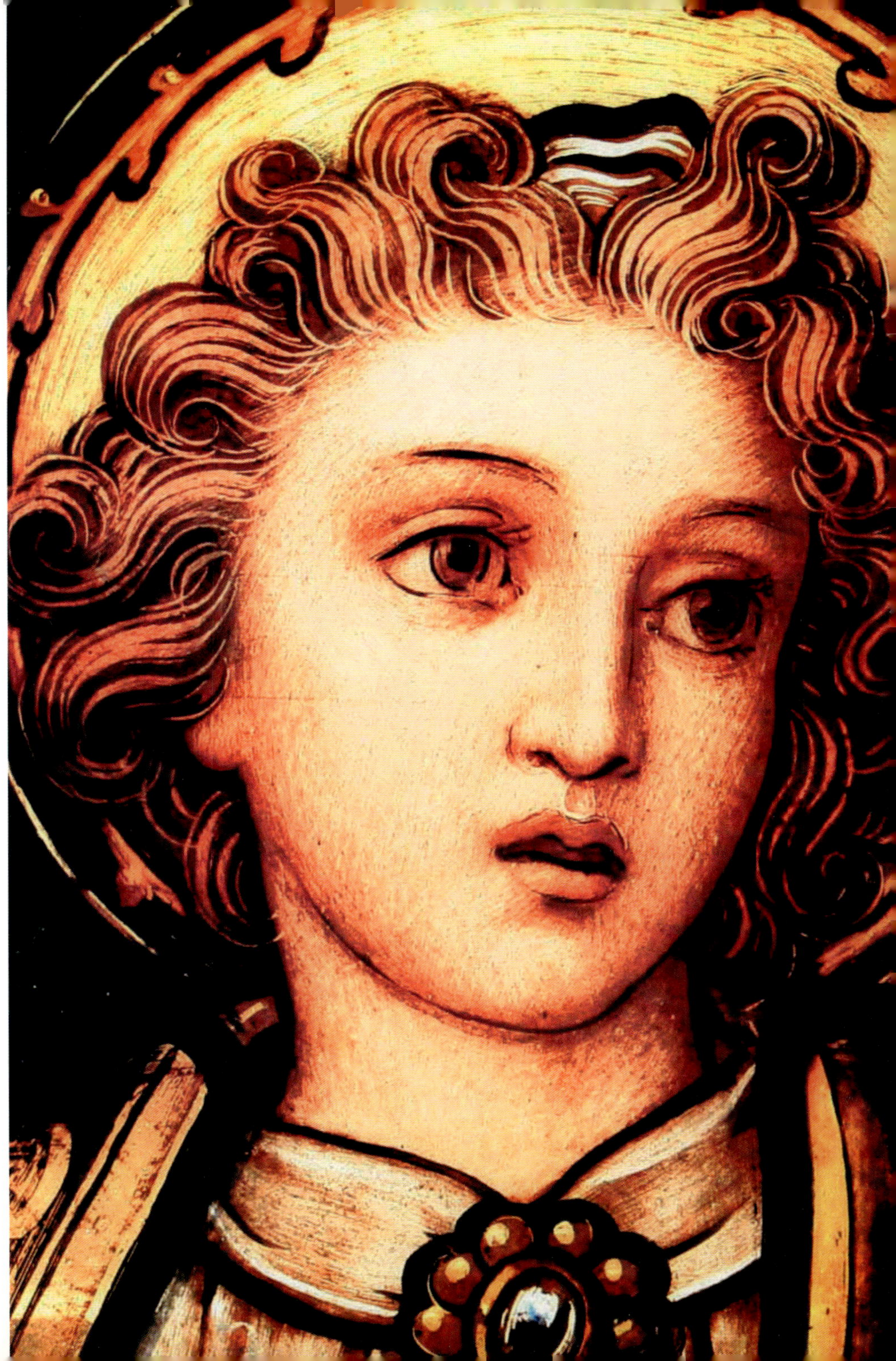

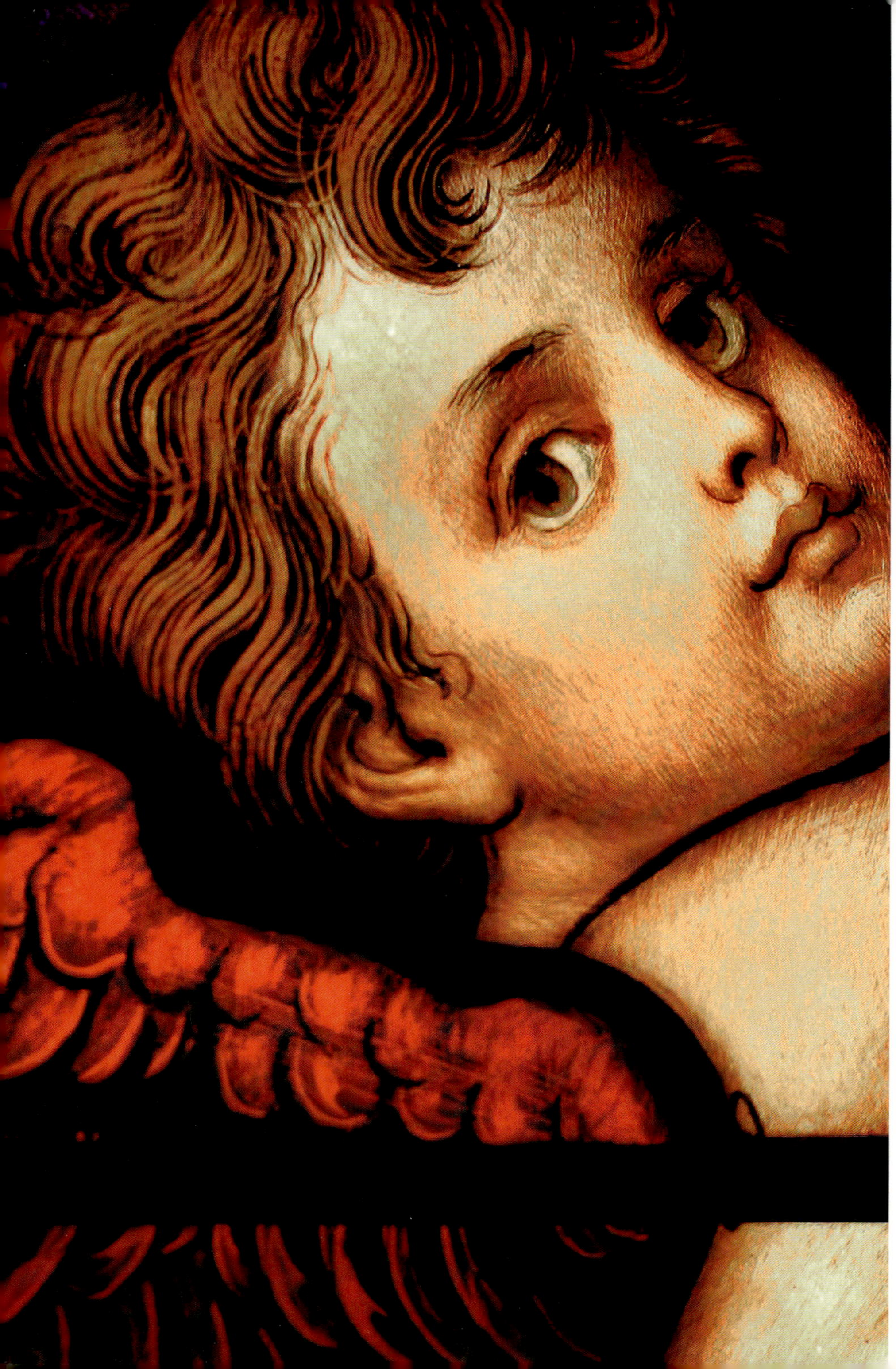

"May God grant you always....
A sunbeam to warm you,
a moonbeam to charm you,
a sheltering Angel so nothing
can harm you.
Laughter to cheer you.
Faithful friends near you.
And whenever you pray,
Heaven to hear you."

Irish Blessing

Index of Locations

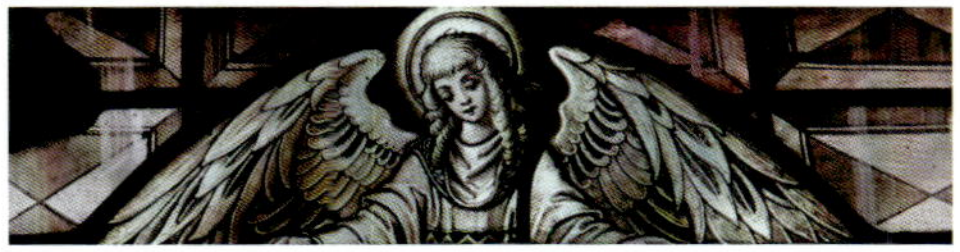

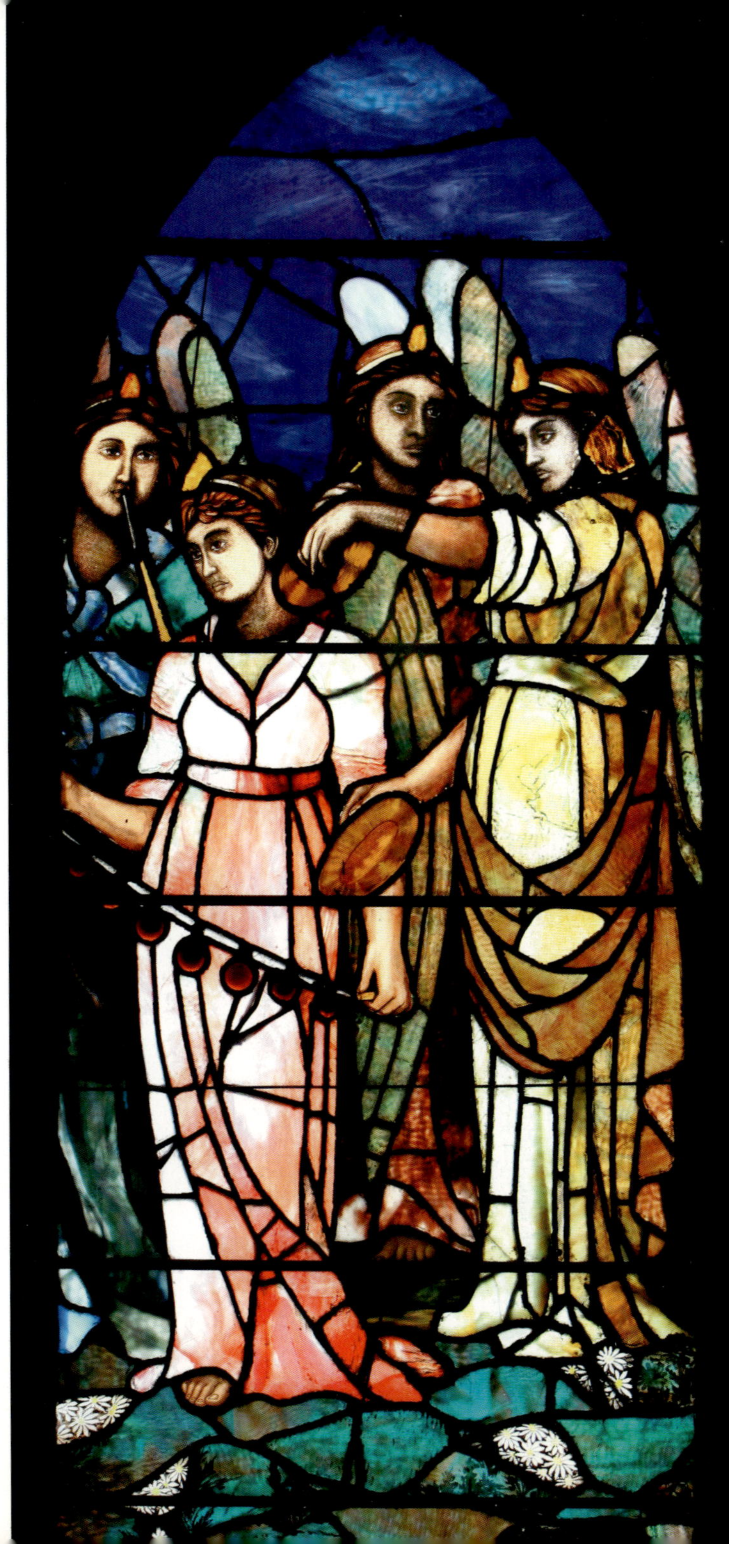

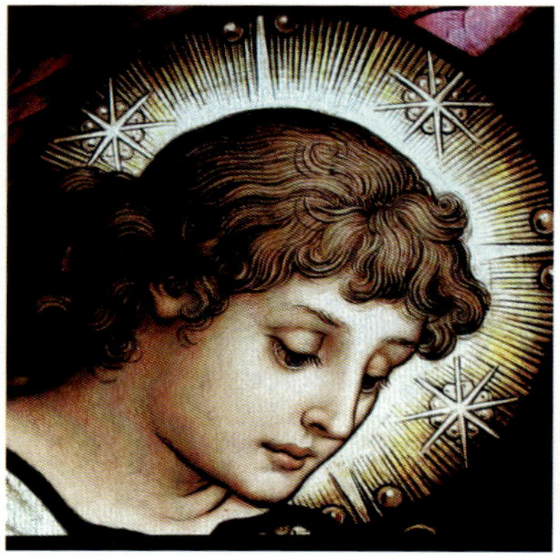
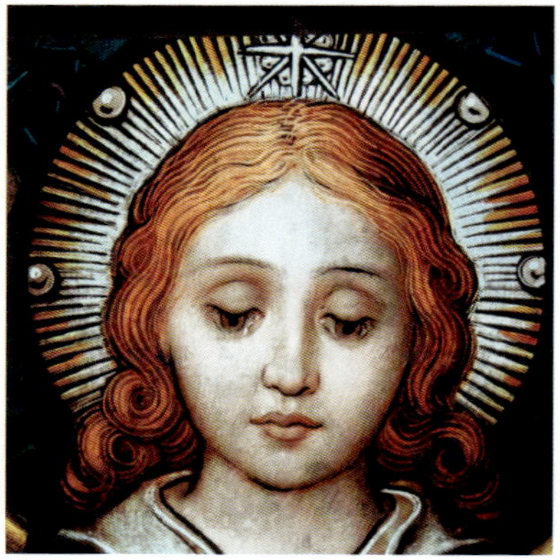
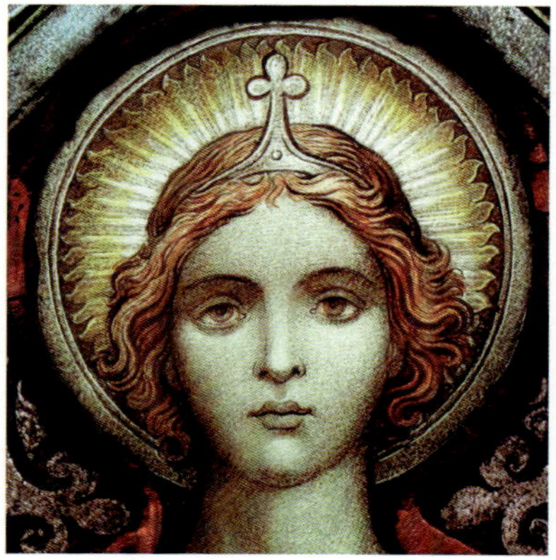
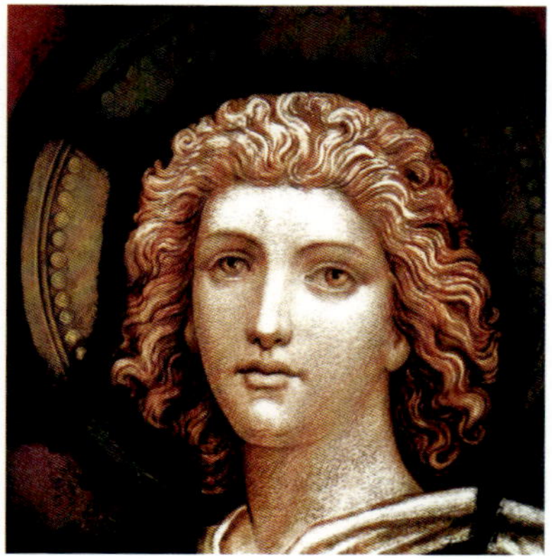

Thanks to all my friends at Indigo Publishing and a special thank you to Tony Long for being an angel in disguise.